Out with the Old, In with the New

Gary Wilson

DEDICATION

'Sons are a heritage from the Lord, children a reward from him.' (Psa. 127:3 NIV).

This book is dedicated to my three children whom I love dearly, Andrew, Sarah and Rachel. You are indeed a blessing and reward from the Lord. This is my written testimony of a God in Jesus Christ who changed my life through His saving love and I leave it as a legacy to you, your children and your children's children.

CONTENTS

ACKNOWLEDGMENTS

I give thanks to the Lord Jesus Christ who delivered me from the kingdom of darkness into his wonderful light.

I thank Liz Dobson for her hours of proof reading, support and encouragement, what a blessing!

I could not have done this without the help of my friend and partner in the Lord, John Caldwell thank you for putting it together and your encouragement to put it into print. I thank the Lord for knowing you my brother.

I thank my wife Helen for her love, support and her faith in the Lord which was and still is a great shining light even in the most challenging times. Many of the stories in this book would not have been possible without Helen.

With all my love always.

FOREWORD

Gary Wilson is a changed man. Once caught in the downward spiral that many slip into (or are born into), he has broken free and has found a path that has taken him onwards and upwards.

Gary expresses the theme of this book perfectly when he writes: "This is an account of a continuous thread of my life moving from the old into the new. Learning from the past but not living in the past."

How is it that a young man can go from a hopeless and hedonistic existence to becoming a passionate follower of Jesus? How does one go from a life of heavy drinking and despair to becoming a minister and having a life full of joy and hope? Gary's primary Bible verse gives us the answer: "Therefore, if anyone is in Christ, he is a new creation. The old has passed away; behold, the new has come." (2 Cor. 5:17).

It's an honour to have been asked by Gary to write this foreword. There is so much in this book that I can personally identify with. I grew up only a few miles from where Gary grew up. As a young man my path followed a similar course of chaos, emptiness and drunkenness. Likewise, I encountered the same Jesus that Gary did, and millions if not billions down through the ages have too. That's the thing about this book, it's a paradox: on the one hand it's Gary's story, but on the other hand it's part of HIS story. It's another chapter in God's great book of redemption. Another life saved and changed by the blood of Jesus Christ. Further, whilst Gary is the main character, this book isn't all about him. The real main character in this story is Jesus. He is the One who leads Gary's steps. He is the one who reveals himself in both the mountain tops and the valleys of Gary's journey.

I feel privileged to be writing this foreword, and it's a privilege to know Gary and indeed many of the people and places he mentions in his book. I lived on Skye for six years, and served alongside Gary for a few years at Skye Bible Church. I now find myself serving God as a minister in the same denomination as Gary. I'm overjoyed that this book has been written because I believe it will not only encourage Christians who read it, but it will help non-Christian readers discover the same Jesus that Gary has. This book will be used by the Lord to both sow seeds and reap a harvest.

One of the things that marks this book, and marks Gary, is its forthright honesty and authenticity. With Gary, what you see is what you get. I've personally been awed by Gary's compassion for both the church and the lost and that compassion spills over the pages of this book. Gary is not a man for doctrinal wrangling, or church politics — he's a man who loves God and people and his desire for his readers is that they discover the same love of God that he has.

Finally, Gary doesn't give the impression that the Christian life is all mountaintops and sunsets. There are moments of miracles, and there is joy and peace and laughter. But there is also pain and sadness. Gary doesn't gloss over this. This is a book about a real person, doing real life, with a real God and that's what makes the difference.

"Out with the old, in with the new" was an old Scottish Hogmanay saying that expressed the hope of a new year. It was "good bye" to the old year with all its pain, and "hello" to the new year with all its hopes and opportunities. In this book, Gary shows us that we can have more than a hope for a better year, we can have a brand new life through faith in Jesus Christ.

Thank you Gary for sharing your journey with us. We are all the richer for it.

John Caldwell, Pastor of Kairos Church

1: OUT WITH THE OLD: IN WITH THE NEW

'Forget the former things; do not dwell on the past. See, I am doing a new thing!' (Isa. 43:18-19).

I start off by looking back at my life up to the present day. It might seem strange to begin with the prophecy of Isaiah where he tells us not to dwell on the past, but what I think he means is do not get stuck in the past, but learn from the past and move on in the present, for if we keep looking back at the so called 'good old days' and long to be back there, we get trapped in the past. Similarly, if we keep looking back to our past mistakes, failures and sin and don't move on in the grace and goodness of God, we get bound to the past. *'See, I am doing a new thing! Now it springs up; do you not perceive it?'* This is an account of a continuous thread of my life moving from the old into the new. Learning from the past but not living in the past. Hope you enjoy my journey!

The phrase 'out with the old, in with the new', was taught to me by mum when I was a young lad growing up in Glasgow.

We started our home life in the tenements of Kilearn Street in Possilpark, up until I was nine years old my dad would have to carry me into the living room, from their bedroom to finish off my sleep every night, as we only had one room and living room in our flat.

We had no shower, no bath, but we had an inside toilet. Our big break came when the Council built new high rise flats in many areas of Glasgow, and we were allocated a new flat in a 16 storey block in Milton, which was about three miles away from Possilpark.

It was luxury when we moved there in 1969. I was given my own personal bedroom, my mum and dad had their own bedroom and we had a living room, kitchen, and toilet with a bath which had the very posh name of bathroom. We lived 15 storeys high and had amazing views of Glasgow. It was on

Hogmanay (New Year's Eve) that my mother opened the windows at couple of minutes before midnight, with the wind blasting in, saying: 'Out with the old, in with the new!'

The old year was passing and the New Year is coming. Welcome in the New Year and it came in with a blast of cold wind. I have never forgotten that phrase, and it became so relevant to me in later life when a dramatic change took place in my life about 20 years later.

I was brought up in the north side of Glasgow. As an only child my mum said that one child was enough as I almost drove her to despair as a baby, crying for almost a year, hence the term of endearment, 'greetin face'. As an only child I had longed for a brother or sister but this never came, however I had a close family with many cousins and friends.

I attended Saracen Primary and remember at my first day at school getting into a fight with another five year old, and the teacher did not hold back by giving us the belt on our legs to break up the fight, we never fought in the class again. I moved to Miltonbank School, and got involved in football and became the goalkeeper for our school team, a very proud moment. I enjoyed school but when it was time to go to high school my confidence took a massive dip, and I did not reach my potential at Colston Secondary, like a lot of pupils who did not do well we were never encouraged.

Yet I found great encouragement when I started to attend the Boys' Brigade, the 277th company. I achieved my Gold award and went on to become an officer in the Brigade. This was all down to a man called Colin O'Brien who took me and my friends under his wing, he spent time with us, encouraged us, challenged us, and made things possible for us to achieve. This was due to his compassion and faith in Jesus which he shared with us in practical and encouraging ways. It was at this period of my life that I heard about God, attended Sunday school, even became a member of the Church of Scotland, but did not have a living relationship with God.

When I was 15, I left school and got a job as an apprentice template-maker working in Fleming Brothers structural engineers in Glasgow. I still attended Boys' Brigade as a young officer, but stopped going to church.

I started to go out with friends to parties and pubs, if we could get into them, and my life started to change. On one occasion I went out with a work friend and we went to a pub called the Saints and Sinners, and by the time I left that establishment, I knew without a shadow of doubt that I was a sinner not a saint.

My friend and I had too much to drink, we were 17 years old at the time, came out of the pub and got into a brawl, we both ended up in the local police cell for a night and went up to face the judge in court the next morning. This was a changing point in my life; as I faced that judge he read out charges to me, and asked if I pled guilty or not guilty. I cannot remember much of what happened. I was found guilty of breach of the peace, and was told by the judge to keep out of trouble for the next year, and face him in court a year later, which I did, and he still gave me a fine of £30. I was ashamed of myself, my poor mum was crying in court to see her only son found guilty.

Just before I finished my trade with Fleming Brothers, I started dating a girl and we got married, I was 21 and she was 19. We set up home in the south side of the city and a couple of years later my firm closed down, meaning that I was made redundant. I remember the government minister saying in a not very helpful way 'get on your bikes and look for a job,' when the country was in the middle of a big recession.

I did get a job working in Craig Nicol

refrigeration as a labourer and stayed with the firm for another five years or so. During this time a major trauma happened in my life; after a few years of marriage my wife left me for someone else and told me that she did not love me anymore, it became one of the darkest periods of my life. I started to drink heavily, got into lots of fights, clubbing every weekend, not always knowing where I had been, what I had done or what had been done to me. It was a scary time and this wild and riotous living lasted for about a year.

I remember at that time I had lost all confidence in relationships and with my own abilities, and I had become a very bitter person. I also did not like myself and would often try to punish my body, by running with a black bin bag under my training gear to sweat out every ounce of fat that I thought I had on me. Looking back, I did not eat properly and was heading in a downward spiral. I did not care if I hurt people, after all I was hurt and nobody cared about me, which was completely false, as I had friends who stood by me and parents who put up with me big time.

It was at one point in my darkest hour that I had had enough of the way I was living my life. I had been on a night out, and somehow managed to get home. I remember waking up in the morning with baked beans all over my face and in my bed not knowing how this had happened. I was lonely, scared at the way my life was going. I was afraid of death as I did not know where my destiny would be after this life, yet the tragedy was the way I was living my life could have led to death. I had all these doubts, fears, anxieties, lack of self- worth, not liking myself and riddled with guilt. I thought, what hope do I have? What is this life all about? Then a thought came into my head, my granny used to read the bible to me, can that help me? I got out the old King James Version and tried to read it, but could not understand the language. I gave up!

The next day, I went to buy a daily newspaper and I saw in an advert 'New Life Bible'. I thought, what is this? I sent away for a copy and it came within two or three days. I started to read it, it was in my language. I could understand some of the words and stories.

I turned to a page and will never forget this, as long as I live, it was this passage God used to change my life. It said: '*If a person be in Christ Jesus they are a new creation the old has gone the new has come!*' (2 Cor. 5:17).

I got strangely excited by reading this, I

asked myself, can I be changed? I have messed up big time. All the sins I have committed, drunkenness, fighting and brawling, divorce, hurting others and blaspheming the name of God. God would surely have no time for me I thought. It was there in my bedroom over 32 years ago, I got on my knees and cried out to God. I was truly sorry for all the sin I had done in my life, I wanted to turn away from this but I needed help. I could not forgive myself, I was bound in condemnation and guilt. I asked God, 'If you are there can you help me? I am desperate! I am sorry! I want a new start! Please forgive me I have sinned against you.'

It was then I experienced a power that I later found out was the Holy Spirit, who flooded my body, mind and spirit with love, forgiveness and great joy. I felt this power go through me, and it was like I was being cleansed and healed and saved in this experience of crying out to God.

I knew from that moment on my life had completely changed. I was a new creation in Christ Jesus. I was born again. I was made new by the love and compassion of God through the saving work of Jesus Christ on the cross, which I was to find out later at a Billy Graham meeting.

This God experience happened to me at

the weekend, and when I went to work on Monday my work friends were asking me what I had got up to at the weekend. I said, 'I met with Jesus, He came into my life, He is real, He is alive and my life has been changed. I can see things differently, I could see God's creation as I came to work this morning, I have never really paid attention to the trees or the beauty of a flower, my eyes have been opened.' You can imagine what kind of reaction I got from my colleagues, suffice to say they thought I had lost it or had been on the wacky baccy!

My life change sat uneasy with some of my friends and family. Some thought that I was just going through a phase and would grow out of it. Others thought that I had become religious, (which I hadn't) many thought I was going weird.

Others probably thought I was foolish giving up my party life, even my desire to earn loads of money.

I remember going out with my friends one evening, we went for a few drinks and on to a club. I had such a great time as I literally danced the night away and was aware of what I was doing. I remember getting home, going to bed, having a great sleep and waking up in the morning without a hangover and was so full of joy. I started to enjoy my life.

I had not become religious, God was developing within me a loving relationship, that was healing my hurts and guiding me in a new and better quality of life! I had heard in the past many negative views about church and Christianity, but I was having such a ball and was so full of joy, I felt I was going to burst with happiness!

However, there was one thing I had not been able to do, that was to go to church. I thought that people in church were all really good people, they had made it life, and they wore nice coats, suits, shirt and tie and were pillars of society.

I never for a moment thought that they would accept someone like me, with my background, my sin and shortcomings, and the life that I once lived. It took me a few weeks to pluck up courage to go, and one Sunday I did. I will never forget the welcome I received from an older couple, they asked me to sit with them and after the service had coffee with me and treated me like a son. Their grace and welcome had such an impact on me that I got involved with the fellowship, and not long after felt that God was calling me to give up my job, house, church and community, to go on a journey with Him in some kind of ministry, as to what, I had no idea at the time.

I had such a close relationship with God, I was living on my own and spent time in His word and prayer, spent time with other Christians and started to grow in my relationship with God. I was finding that God was changing me and challenging me to let go of the past and let God lead and direct me. The word says: '*Do not conform any longer to the pattern of this world, but be transformed by the renewing of your mind*' (Rom. 12:2). God was not only renewing my heart but also my mind, my attitude and thought patterns.

I used to be quite a negative person, quite a gossip, self-centred and not very nice to be around. I always wanted to be in control of my life, to earn lots of money, have a good home, car and the latest gadgets. All these things in themselves are not bad but materialism had got a grip of my life. God in His grace was challenging me to see how much I trusted Him. On one occasion after reading the bible and seeing the plight of some of the poverty stricken people in Africa, I felt the Holy Spirit was prompting me to give some of my savings to the ministry of Tearfund.

I wrestled with this for about a week and I had no peace, as I was still holding onto these material riches. I remember saying: 'Lord if you want me to give all my savings to Tearfund and the work in Africa I will do it but please provide for me, not my wants, but my daily needs.' After a mammoth struggle I sent a cheque to Tearfund for all my savings, I felt such a peace as I was now trusting God to provide for me.

About a week later I got a wonderful letter from Tearfund thanking me for the donation, and I think it was either the same day or day later, I received a cheque through the post for more than I had given away.

I was awe struck by the provision of the Lord. It was very timely as my life was about to start out on a new journey, one that would completely change my life again!

The call to go and leave the familiar behind.

By now I was really experiencing a strong call from God to leave my home, job, and city to go on a journey that the Lord would open up for me one step at a time. However, I was not sure what it was I was being called to. So one day I found the phone number of the Church of Scotland offices in Edinburgh and asked to speak to someone, I was put through to a very wise minister who asked me the reason for the call. I answered: 'I believe God is calling me to do something for

Him but I don't know what. I am happy to serve! Maybe I've to go to India, Africa or stay at home to share the gospel.'

He arranged to meet up with me and as we met a week later, he encouraged me to go and volunteer at my local church for one year, visit the elderly, get involved with Sunday school, and get to meet people in the congregation to see how God would lead me in the next year.

Also, as I had no educational qualifications, to study an English higher at college. This was great advice and I got heavily involved with the congregation at Kings Park parish church working under Rev Stewart Smith. I decided to do an O-grade English qualification at college and also enrolled to do a bible course on 'How to preach!' I loved the 'How to preach' course but struggled with the O-grade English, however I kept going for the next year.

I was feeling that my calling was getting stronger and I contacted my ministry friend who had advised me the year before, he suggested that I apply to the Church of Scotland to become a parish assistant, I duly got the application form and applied. The major problem that I could see from the application form was that I needed higher English, which I did not have, but I committed it to the Lord and submitted my form.

A few weeks later I was given an invitation to attend an interview at Carberry Tower near Edinburgh. Before I attended the interview I found out that I had failed my English O-level, however, I passed my 'How to preach' course.

I thought to myself, it looks like I won't get to be a parish assistant as I have no English qualifications, but the Lord knows better than me.

I went to the interview and was asked a series of questions. I had to admit to the Board I had failed English but passed my preaching course, and they thanked me for coming and said they would be in touch.

About a week later I received a letter saying that I had been accepted to train for a parish assistant, and would need to attend a residential college called St Colm's, for two years in Edinburgh. I was stunned, excited and very thankful that God had opened this door for me. It now meant that the time had come to move on, to sell my house, to leave my job, and the hardest thing of all to leave my mum, dad, friends and Glasgow to go to Edinburgh!

It was at this point the reality of this new opportunity started to sink in. Was I doing the right thing? People were saying I was silly to sell my house. But the Lord kept reassuring me that He was in this and He would provide as He had done in the past.

I gave notice to my work that I was leaving in September, I put my house up for sale and it sold within a very short time, I moved back in with my parents and then set out with much trepidation on this new adventure, out with the old - in with the new!

I arrived at St Colm's college in Edinburgh at the start of September 1989 for a two year residential course, which was a mixture of bible study, practical theology, church placements and living in a community with about 20 other students. This was a massive change for me, for it was no longer looking after Number One, but being part of a community of people taking turns at running the house, cleaning, washing, doing dishes, as well as trying to get to know a whole group of people I had never met before. Many of them found it hard to understand my strong Glaswegian language, and I was desperately trying to learn new English words to communicate with my student group that included people from Africa, Pakistan, India, Chile, USA, Italy, Edinburgh and one other Glaswegian. St

Colm's was a great place for me to learn much about the Lord, myself and others.

My first church placement was at a very wealthy church called Murrayfield Parish. I certainly felt out of my depth in that congregation. Although the people were very nice to me I felt quite intimidated by many who were of professional class, doctors, lecturers, teachers, professors and many more.

One Sunday I read the scriptures at the morning service, and a lady came up and said to me it was good to hear a Scottish voice reading the bible. Another memory was when I was standing at the door with the minister shaking people's hands as they left church, to my horror I looked down at my shoes which were lovely and shiny, the sole had started to come away from the right foot, so I put my left foot on top of it to hide it, and then other sole started to come away. I think I got away with it, and I don't know how I got home with my feet hanging out of my shoes.

Looks are deceiving, these shoes were handed down to me from my grandad and looked good but they were shiny plastic, probably picked up from the Barras in Glasgow.

The Murrayfield experience was a

challenge but a good one!

Year one was coming to end at St Colm's and I surprised myself by getting a pass in my first year, and the offer to continue with year two. However that was another four months away, what should I do over the summer? God opened another new opportunity to go to Israel for three months...

2: ISRAEL – HERE I COME!

It was one thing to go to Edinburgh to study, and another to go to Israel. I had been given the wonderful opportunity to go and work at the Church of Scotland Hospice in Tiberias on the Sea of Galilee, along with a few other students from Scotland.

The Hospice was originally a mission hospital and had now become a place of hospitality where pilgrims could go and spend time in the Land. When I spoke to my mum about my new opportunity for the summer she was worried and said: 'How is it you are going to all the places where there are bombings and killings?'

I had been a few months earlier on a visit

to Belfast with some of my new college friends, at the time of the troubles, now I was having to travel to Israel via London, which my mum was quite worried about. My answer was: 'God will protect and guide me in His ways, I trust that this is what He wants for me.'

This was a challenge for me to leave the comforts of home even though it was only for three months, again to work in a new environment with a whole bunch of people, but it was to become one of the richest spiritual experiences of my life.

I arrived and started work at the Scottish Hospice in Tiberias. After the first day I ended up in a darkened bedroom for 24 hours, as I had succumbed to sunstroke and was dehydrated.

The temperature was 40 degrees Celsius and the heat and humidity was oppressive, it took me a good week to acclimatise to the new conditions. One of the ways we would cool off was swimming in the beautiful fresh water lake which is called the Sea of Galilee. It was so surreal to be swimming in the lake, where Jesus calmed the storm, where the disciples had a miraculous catch of fish when their nets were almost torn with such a vast amount.

I spent 10 weeks working at the centre

doing various jobs and visiting places; like Jerusalem, Bethlehem, Capernaum, Nazareth, Cana, Jaffa and many, many more places that were mentioned in the bible.

One of the most amazing places was the Garden Tomb in Jerusalem, the place of Jesus' resurrection. My bible became alive in a different way through having the experience of seeing the places where Jesus ministered, and the place called Gethsemane and Golgotha where He endured the cross. I also met many beautiful people of the Land, Palestinian Christians, Jewish people, Arabs, Druze to name but a few. They were all warm and welcoming peoples, none more so than a man called Hanna Azar from Bethlehem who worked as a cook in the church centre in Jerusalem. We became great friends and he gave me a great insight to the land and politics. He was a humble Christian brother who did not find it easy living in Bethlehem, which was changing from being predominately Christian to a having a bigger Muslim influx as many Palestinian Christians were leaving the Land. I was to reunite with brother Hanna again, a year later, which is another story.

During this time the news was full of Saddam Hussein's attack on Kuwait and the beginning of the Gulf War.

Rumours spread every day that he was about to launch scud missiles against Israel and they would be heading into Israel's northern border not far from where we were. Some people started to cut their time short in the Land by heading home, the majority of us stayed on to fulfil our time. It was at one Sunday evening service at Tiberias, I was part of the singing group, and we were praising the Lord looking over the Sea of Galilee singing: 'Great is Thy faithfulness O God my Father….. morning by morning new mercies I see, all I have needed Thy hand has provided, great is Thy faithfulness, Lord unto me!' God is faithful and we were not aware of any missile attacks at the time we were in the Land and I believe to this day no bomb has landed on that church centre.

My time in Israel was coming to an end, and I had a broader picture of Christian service and Christian faith in the land where my Saviour Jesus had spent 33 years of his earthly life, before His resurrection and ascension back into heaven sitting at the right hand of the Father. God was taking me on a journey that was constantly challenging and changing and leading me to a surprising door that He would open for me into full time ministry in the years ahead!

As the song goes: 'Ah, Lord God you have

made the heavens and the earth by your great power! Nothing is too difficult for you, nothing is too difficult for you! O, great and mighty God, great in power and mighty in deed, nothing, nothing, absolutely nothing, nothing is too difficult for you.'

I arrived back into Glasgow with a longing to return to the Land someday as something about Israel and its people had touched me deeply. I had a love for the people and the Land which has lasted to this very day. I had no idea that the next year ahead would be one of a major and significant change in my life again as I went back to college in Edinburgh for my second year: '*Forget the former things do not dwell in the past see I am doing a new thing! Now it springs up; do you not perceive it?*' Learn from the past, don't live in the past!

The journey continues...

The second year of my studies started in September and a new placement was given to every student, my placement was to be at Wester Hailes a notoriously rough district with many social problems in the area.

The church was Holy Trinity and it had a team ministry consisting of Stan Brook the parish minister, John Collard the associate and Mary Deacons the parish assistant. I wasn't too enthusiastic about going there as I did not think I would have much to do; see I was in the old Presbyterian mind-set of the one-man ministry.

Holy Trinity was to be the most enriching and life changing experiences that I would have in my time at St Colm's. I met with Stan Brook and he sat me down and looked at me and said, 'Gary, I pray that God will richly bless your time here with us.'

No one had ever spoke to me like that before, there was a real love and care for me that I had never experienced before.

My first Sunday at Holy Trinity was electric, I had never been to a church like it. People turned up in their jeans, T-shirts, as well as suits, ties etc. There were many young people, children and people of my age, as well as older folk, an amazing cross section of all ages.

When the service started and the worship band started singing contemporary worship songs, I experienced the same move of the Holy Spirit in my life as I had a few years ago at my meeting with the Lord Jesus.

This place was electrifying, happy, and the power of God was very real in the place. The preacher came out to preach and I had never quite heard anything like it before, so relevant, so powerful, so captivating that I was rejoicing! I went back to college and my tutor asked how I had got on at Holy Trinity, I said,

'It was amazing! I could feel the presence of the Lord very strongly in the worship.'

She said, 'Do you not feel that in every other church?'

'Not really.' I have never experienced such a power of God's presence before in any other church I had been to.

During this second year I started an access course at Edinburgh University called church reformation history, my friend and I felt it would be good to do this together as it interested us and helped us in our studies, it was a night school course, this course would be significant in closing one door and opening another in my journey with God.

I was coming near to the end of my second year and was very reluctant to leave Holy Trinity, which was due to a couple of things, I loved the people and style of worship and I had met the love of my life, a beautiful young woman called Helen Ackford.

It was during an evening service that God brought us together, little did I know that Helen had been praying for a Christian husband for almost 10 years and after the service I had noticed she had been upset. I really did fancy her but I was quite slow in making my feelings known in case she did not like me, however I felt compelled this particular evening to go and talk with her and invite her out, which I eventually did and she accepted and we went on our first date the week before Valentine's Day.

Within a very short time we both knew that the Lord had called us to be together and within six weeks we were engaged to be married, something we would plan at Dunvegan on the Isle of Skye, next to the church that I would eventually become minister, almost nine years later.

I also received another big shock when I heard that I had passed my access course at university, the only test that I had ever passed in my life up to that point was my driving test. Meanwhile as this was happening I was being offered a new full time position to be a parish assistant in St Margaret's church Greenock. I had also had been offered a place at Edinburgh University at New College to study for a Licentiate of Theology. I had a massive decision to make, what would you have me do Lord? Edinburgh or Greenock?

Much prayer and discussions with

Christian friends and my new fiancé, and guidance from my minister helped me along the way. Helen I visited the church at Greenock, met the minister and his wife, saw around the area, we were still not sure.

Many people by this time were encouraging me to go in for the ministry and although I had a place at university I would still have to go through the church's selection school.

After a while we felt it was right to stay in Edinburgh and go to university and trust that God was wanting me to pursue the ministry.

Israel: Jerusalem

As I felt the calling of the Lord to pursue the path of more study and to make application for the ministry, I had also applied to go back to work in Israel again over the summer months. I had been accepted to go and work at the St Andrew's Hospice in Jerusalem, this was to be a challenging time for me as I was leaving my fiancé behind for the next 10 weeks.

As soon as I arrived in Jerusalem I was homesick for my Helen and I did not think I could feel as bad as I did. I found it so hard to concentrate and settle, the saving grace was that Helen was coming out to visit Israel and me in two weeks' time.

I managed to calm down a bit and get on with what I was meant to be doing, working at the reception, boing a waiter, gardener and a host of other things. My accommodation was in the ancient church tower which had amazing views of the old city of Jerusalem. As the psalmist wrote: '*I rejoiced with those who said to me "Let us go to the house of the Lord." Our feet are standing in your gates, O Jerusalem.... Like a city built together where the people of God go up to praise the name of the Lord.*' (Psa. 122: 1-4). I had the privilege every morning waking up to the view of the old city, the ancient citadel of King David and undoubtedly the place where Jesus would enter and teach the people about the ushering in of the kingdom of God; where the blind would see, the lame walk and the captives be set free. I met a mixture of people and caught up with my Palestinian friend Hanna. I also got friendly with a Jewish rabbi from the USA who was a guest at the hospice, he bought me a little skull cap as a gift because one day he asked if I would take him up the church tower to see over the old city, it was a very windy day and he said,

'Is there anything to hold on to up there?'

'Yes, my brother, built into the top of the tower is the cross and you can always hold on to that!'

The time came for me to go and collect Helen from the airport in Tel Aviv, called Ben Gurion, named after the first Prime Minister of the modern state of Israel. I had to drive on their crazy roads, I thank God I lived to tell the story. As I was waiting for Helen to come into the arrival lounge, I was transfixed by this little Jewish boy, he had his little skull cap on and he was holding on to his mum, he was very excited and I could make out that he was so looking forward to seeing his dad. He saw his dad come through into the arrival lounge and he cried: 'Abba! Abba!' meaning 'Father! Father!'

He ran towards him, but his dad was running towards him with open arms and lifted him, hugged and embraced him. I was in tears! It reminded me of the story of the prodigal son and the welcome that the wayward son received as he made his way back to his father.

'How great is the love the Father has lavished on us, that we should be called children of God! And that is what we are.' (1

Jn. 3:1).

What a wonderful picture of the Father's love that I was witnessing in Tel Aviv airport between a father and his son.

Helen eventually arrived and we set on our way driving the ancient road up to Jerusalem. For the next two weeks we would visit much of the land and meet many hospitable people.

My friend Hanna, invited us to go for lunch at his family home in Bethlehem to meet his wife and family. We were treated like royalty and given a banquet of local Palestinian food, stuffed vine leaves, fruits, Turkish coffee, the works. Hanna showed us round this significant city, he took us to the site where they believe Jesus was born, then on to the nearby Shepherds Field. Bethlehem which was noisy, vibrant, and full of smells, hustle and bustle and not what I thought it would be like according to the pictures on our Christmas cards. We travelled north to Tiberias which is situated on the edge of the Sea of Galilee, we visited the Scots hospice where I had worked the previous year, toured around the villages of Capernaum, Tabgha, Mount of Beatitudes, Caesarea Philippi, on towards the majestic heights of Mount Hermon where we reached the top of the summit via a ski lift.

The next day we headed back to Jerusalem on route to the Dead Sea the lowest point in the world, where we floated, looking over to the mountains of Moab. The Dead Sea has no life in it all due to the quantities of salt in the water, yet this is the very place where according to the prophet Ezekiel, that the river of God would flow from the temple in Jerusalem all the way down to the Dead Sea, where it would become fresh water, living water that would bring life. For wherever the river flows it will bring life. (Eze. 47).

This experience of being in Israel taught me so much, and being at the Dead Sea revealed to me that though things can look dead and of no use God can bring life to the dead, whether it be the dry bones of the House of Israel, the Dead Sea, or the empty tomb in Jerusalem with the words on the tomb door; 'He is not here, He is Risen! Hallelujah!' Wherever the river of God flows it brings life, new life, revived, restored, and resurrected life!

It was time for Helen to fly back home to Scotland and it was the hardest thing to take her to the airport and not go home with her, suffice to say that I only managed to last another two or three weeks before I flew back to Scotland.

I felt guilty at not staying the full 10 weeks and struggled with the decision I had made, I felt I had let other staff members down and that I had even let God down. One Jewish lady who was staying at the centre said to me when I was sharing about how I felt, 'Gary, no one is indispensable,' and she was right. I still however went home feeling as if I had failed, but happy to see Helen.

3: SOMETHING OLD, SOMETHING NEW! MARRIAGE

Helen and I visited the Isle of Skye, and as we were touring around the island we stopped at Dunvegan, not far from the Church of Scotland, and started to plan the date of our wedding which we decided would be on 28th March 1992 at Holy Trinity Church, Wester Hailes. When I look back it was quite amazing that we planned our big day at the place where nine years later I would be called to be the minister of that large parish. We went back to Edinburgh full of excitement to share our news and to prepare for that big day. I was about to start at New College, and a young couple offered me accommodation for the next few months up until our wedding day.

It was getting near to our big day, the 28th March, which we had longed for over the past year. Our coming together was pretty miraculous when you think about it. Helen was born in Devon, and moved around many countries due to her father's work, before coming back to this country.

She had spent a good number of years living in Hong Kong, and when her schooling finished she visited a few universities in the UK, and was given an offer to study Biology at Edinburgh University.

She moved to Edinburgh, from Hong Kong, and was very much on her own, the rest of her family lived in Devon. Helen had a friend who invited her to church one Sunday and she decided to take up the offer. At that service in Holy Trinity she heard the gospel and was drawn to Jesus, and the love of a heavenly Father who was with her. This had such an impact on her, as her mum and dad were overseas, and her brother and rest of family were in and around the West Country. Later that night she gave her life to the Lord and was born again, and became a member at Holy Trinity and got heavily involved in many aspects of church life.

I, to this day, find it incredible that the

Lord brought us together in His perfect timing, as we had lived in different parts of the world and came from very different family backgrounds.

Our union was built on our relationship with God; our background and status does not matter, we are all equal in the eyes of God.

The wedding day arrived and I had brunch with the young couple who had let me stay with them. I went out to get something about two hours before the wedding, and I was going past the hotel where our reception was to be and saw a coach pulling in. It was all my family and friends arriving from Glasgow, and I was getting big hugs and pictures taken, and I wasn't even in my wedding clothes. I had to tear myself away as I was meeting my best man Tom, and we had to get ready. I was in such a rush; Helen always reminds me that I forgot to brush my hair!

We arrived at church and it was packed. The praise band were playing some songs and then the bridal music started, and my Helen came down the aisle with her dad, she looked beautiful, stunning, I was overwhelmed. The first hymn started called: Praise to the Lord the Almighty the king of creation. I could barely sing as I was overcome with emotion and the tears started to flow, I was thanking God for his goodness to me and blessing me with a wonderful friend and wife.

It was the happiest day of my life. Our dear friend Heather read the following words of scripture: *'And I pray that you, being rooted and established in love, may have power, together with all the saints, to grasp how wide and long and high and deep is the love of Christ, and to know this love that surpasses knowledge – that you may be filled to the measure of all the fullness of God. Now to him who is able to do immeasurably more than all we ask or imagine, according to his great power that is at work within us, to him be glory in the church and in Christ Jesus throughout all generations, for ever and ever! Amen.'* (Eph. 3:17-21).

Our marriage was the beginning of a team ministry that Helen and I would embark on together, in the love and great power of the One who called us together. I still had another three years at university to do, but before that we headed off to the Isle of Skye for our honeymoon. This new covenant of marriage that we entered into, is not just a partnership, it is more. A covenant is a strong and binding tie that we have of love and loyalty for one another, sealed by the blessing of God. Our trip to Skye was truly wonderful, and it would be in the future the place that the Lord would bring us back to in the years ahead.

New College

The day I started at the School of Divinity, New College I immediately felt out of my depth. I did not talk as well as the other students, I certainly did not have the qualifications that many of them had, and I found the first term extremely difficult. On a few occasions I believed that I had made a big mistake by starting at university and giving up a full time parish assistant post. The essays were difficult, I was staying up to the wee hours in the morning trying to finish these assignments and barely passing the mark. With my first essay I achieved 26/50. I went to my tutor and said,

'What do you want from me, blood? I have given everything to this piece of work and only just passed.'

'Well at least you passed,' he said, and then he went on to teach me how to answer the questions properly, the penny finally dropped and I got into the work and started to enjoy the course.

During this time I felt prompted to apply

for the ministry Selection School to test if I had a calling to the ministry.

Yes, I was at university but I still did not have an English qualification to my name, I had come from a broken marriage, had been a drunkard, had been in a prison cell for a night and had a breach of the peace conviction; I had also left Jerusalem four weeks early, things on paper did not look too good for me. I prayed; 'Lord may your will be done; I don't feel too confident at going to the selection school but please have your way, in Jesus name.'

The Selection School was a two day event and a number of other candidates were being tested. It was quite intense and challenging. With interviews with the Board of Ministry, interview with a psychologist and various scenarios and a three minute talk - all had their difficulties. I think we all left that school drained and were told we would be notified in due course. It was about a week later that I received the letter and I opened it and was overwhelmed by what I read, that I had been selected as a candidate in training for the ministry of the Church of Scotland, and would do a period of four years at university along with church placements.

I was ecstatic! 'Thank you, Lord! You are so good Lord, how could I ever doubt you. To you be the glory and honour and praise!'

I was now a student in training for the ministry. As well as doing my degree, I had two placements over the four years, my first was in St Colm's, Dalry, working with a Rev Stewart MacPherson. It was a new church that was built within a sheltered housing complex.

On one occasion I was to conduct the whole service and be assessed by a minister sent from the Board of Ministry. I stood up to start the service, and I saw this scruffy looking guy wearing a kilt, combat jacket, Doc Martins, and with long hair that looked as if it hadn't been washed for months, accompanied by a scruffy wee dog. He sat near the back of the church and I could see people moving to keep out of his way. After the service not everyone was very kind or welcoming to him, some said he had nits in his hair. I went to meet with the minister and elders to get their feedback about my leading of the service, again the strange man who had come into church did not receive many kind words, even from the elders, some were asking who was this guy? and why was he here? I addressed the elders and said:

'That was my lecturer of New Testament studies at Edinburgh University who is a Doctor of Divinity and also an ordained

Church of Scotland minister and he was here to assess my leading of worship.'

I think many of them were embarrassed and did not know what to say and left the building without saying a word. This taught me something, that we should be a people and church who welcome other people no matter what their background, what they wear, even if they are different from us, we have to show love and care for all who come into the house of God. Jesus spoke to the religious who asked him: *'Of all the commandments, which is the most important?' "The most important one," answered Jesus, "is this: 'Hear, O Israel, the Lord our God, the Lord is one. Love the Lord your God with all your heart and with all your soul and with all your mind and with all your strength.' The second is this: 'Love your neighbour as yourself.' There is no commandment greater than these."* (Mk. 12:28-30).

My second placement was at Gorgie Parish Church, under the mentorship of Rev David Anderson who was a wonderful man of God.

He gave me plenty of opportunities to serve, and take part in the congregational life of the church being involved in preaching, leading prayer meetings and parish visiting. It was during this time that we formed a very good friendship with Colin and Fiona Cuthill who ran the youth group. It was during this learning experience that David called me into his office one day and gave me an encouraging word from the Lord. He said, ' I don't often get these experiences but I want to share something from the Lord with you, I believe you are to be a different kind of church minister, not the usual ordained minister, but one who is to be an evangelist.'

I was moved that David would think about me and receive a word from God for me, later this message would be fulfilled by another confirmation of that word by a man from the other side of the planet. I thank God for David and his family, they took both Helen and I very much into their lives and blessed us greatly.

During this time I had become a member at Holy Trinity Church.

Helen and I served in a youth ministry together, and had a wonderful group of young people who loved the Lord and who had a love to reach out to the many broken young people of Wester Hailes.

It was round about this time that a fresh wind of God's Holy Spirit was touching many people. We went to a few meetings that were happening at Holy Trinity and they had a visiting speaker from New Zealand called Tony Walker. The meeting was very powerful and people were going forward and being prayed for, some were falling to the ground under the power of the Holy Spirit and were prophesying, speaking in tongues, singing, laughing, and this was not what I was used to. I must admit I was quite sceptical of what was going on, I did not go forward for prayer, and went home.

I went back the next evening and was still in my judgemental mode, when the speaker announced that someone had been given a word that they were an evangelist and that they were to come forward for prayer.

This was exactly the word given to me by my good friend David Anderson, a few months earlier.

I knew I had to go forward, my heart was beating faster, and the Spirit was bubbling up inside of me. The speaker put his hand on my head and I pushed my head forward and he asked what I was doing? I said, that I did not want him to push me down like the rest of those people. He replied, 'I don't push people down, I pray for people and whatever the Holy Spirit wants to do He does.'

As he prayed for me I felt a surge of power go through me, I could not stand and I ended up on the floor, in complete peace, I don't know how long I was on the floor but I was praising the Lord and I just wanted to stay there all night. The presence of the Holy Spirit was heavy.

I remember looking over to Helen and asked the Lord to fill her with the power of the Holy Spirit, I noticed that someone prayed for her, and then she was slain in the Spirit and joined me on the floor. I believe that the Lord was preparing us for the ministry that He was calling us to in the future, I also believe that He was humbling us to rely more on Him and less on ourselves.

After I got up and went home, the next day, I was praying and praising the Lord and I had run out of words to say to my heavenly Father and another language came out of me, heavenly language that I did not understand, but it enabled me to have a closeness with the Lord. It was very much for my spiritual upbuilding as God prepared me for my course and ministry ahead. I later found out that what I had experienced was a baptism of the Holy Spirit, quite similar to what happened to the apostles on the day of Pentecost. *'Suddenly a sound like the blowing of a violent wind came from heaven and filled the whole house where they were sitting. They saw what seemed to be tongues of fire that separated and came to rest on each of them. All of them were filled with the Holy Spirit and began to speak in other tongues as the Spirit enabled them.'* (Acts 2:2-4). Although I did not see tongues of fire or feel a violent wind, I did experience the movement of the wind of the Spirit internally that changed my life, my way of thinking, praying, praising and worship.

I wanted more, I remember missing a theology lecture to go to an afternoon meeting for ministers at a church near the university.

The preacher was talking about the move of the Holy Spirit and how it was touching many ministers of various denominations, bringing a spiritual and physical release to their ministry, which was also having an impact on many local congregations.

Joint prayer meetings were happening through the city and precious unity between some denominations was forming. It was an exciting time. When the minister stopped speaking he called on the Holy Spirit to come and fill people afresh, many started to shake, to cry out, to laugh and to fall to the floor.

I wanted more but nothing seemed to happen to me like it did at the last meeting, I was asking myself have I done something wrong? Then the Lord gave me a picture of the cross, with Jesus on it weeping over His people and the word that was imparted to me was:

'Tell my people that I love them. Wherever you preach tell my people I love them and I weep over them tears of revival for, *if my people, who are called by my name, will humble themselves and pray and seek my face and turn from their wicked ways, then will I hear from heaven and forgive their sin and heal their land.'* (2 Chr. 7:14).

I believe that this was my anointing from the Lord to go in the gifting of an evangelist and tell people about God's love displayed on the cruel cross at Calvary; as Jesus had gave me hope and a new beginning through His love and forgiveness, I had this life giving message of God's love to share with all people, everywhere the Lord would take me. That experience was about 27 years ago and I have been privileged to share the gospel of God's love in Jesus to many people over the years, and still do as I write this.

'To God be the glory, great things He has done, so loved He the world that He gave us His son, who yielded His life an atonement for sin and opened the life gate that all may go in. Praise the Lord!' (Fanny Crosby).

This movement of the Holy Spirit

produced such a change in our worship services, people were being healed, saved and baptised in the Spirit in nearly every time of worship. I remember on one occasion we were out on the streets of Wester Hailes sharing the gospel of Jesus, through our testimonies and were inviting some young folk into the meeting.

A few young folk came in and one lad was so uncomfortable, he said: 'There is something powerful in this place!'

He wanted out, he had been involved with drugs and the occult and was visibly shaking with the power of God, he actually freaked out and left, he could not handle this power. Young people were getting filled with the Holy Spirit as well as older people.

My time at Holy Trinity church was the most rich and rewarding time of my life and it was also the place where God gave me my wife. My wife Helen came with a flat and a full time job working with the Medical Research Council and I came with a car and grant into our marriage, and she supported me for the last three years of my studies.

It was during that time Helen became pregnant with what was to be our first born son Andrew. Andrew was born in 1995 with great joy. We believe that the Lord had blessed us with this little baby. Before Helen knew she was expecting the Lord gave us a word from Psalm 126:3 *'The Lord has done great things for us and we are filled with joy.'*

This was the same day that she went to the doctors to see if she was pregnant or not. She was, and we were filled with Joy.

When Andrew was born nine months later, our first Sunday back at church with our new baby the words of Psalm 126 were put up on the screen with a picture of a bundle of joy. We were overwhelmed once again by the goodness of our God to us.

It was May when Andrew was born, I was finishing at New College and had to submit two essays, one called the Disruption 1843 when the Free Church came out of the Church of Scotland. My proof reader was Helen and she read my essay in the hospital after giving birth to our son, which was a major disruption in itself. I passed all my courses with much help from Helen, especially in the essay department, and I was to be awarded a Bachelor of Divinity with merit, and I still did not have an English qualification to my name.

So much was happening in this short period of time, as I was also meeting with the Board of Ministry who would interview me for my next part of training as an assistant minister for 18 months, working with a congregation and minister who would oversee my training. I was offered three churches to consider, one that we could not even find on the map.

But a year earlier we had been back on Skye, and after a morning service in Portree we met with John Ferguson to ask if he would take an assistant, and he said: 'I will need to test you.'

We were invited to his manse and I went dressed up in my shirt and tie and was ready for an interview, which I never really got, but with a wink of the eye he said,

'Do you like herring?'

I said, 'Does it have bones?'

'Yes, many bones. If you eat the herring you can apply to be my assistant.'

Well, I ate every bit of it – an achievement, considering I don't usually like fish.

I was still waiting for an interview, and he again pulled the rug from under me by saying he was having a house meeting at the manse that night and it would be good if I shared my testimony.

I loved John's interview technique; he got to know everything about me without asking, but just listening as I shared my testimony.

I had shared with the Board of Ministry that I felt God was calling me to go to Skye.

They thought about it and asked me to consider Broadford. I felt deep within me it was to be Portree, and I asked about going there. They said that might not be possible as it was a Gaelic desirable charge and they said they would look into it and left it at that. A few days later I heard from the Board that they would open the way for me to go to Portree for my probationary period.

I was duly licensed to preach the gospel at St Giles' Cathedral, 1 along with other assistant ministers, in a quite moving ceremony, where all my family and friends had gathered with my wee baby son making himself known with a few little cries which rang around this big ancient cathedral. The Lord has indeed done great things for us and we are filled with joy!

4: NEW JOURNEY - OVER THE SEA TO SKYE

We left Edinburgh on the first day of July, to head for Portree with a real sense of excitement and anticipation of taking up my new role as assistant minister of Portree Parish Church. We were very kindly given a house to rent by Andy MacPherson who was the session clerk of the church, this house was about two miles from the village of Portree called Torvaig. It was at the very end of the road, and when we got out of the car and walked for a few yards we were overwhelmed by the stunning views of Ben Tianavaig and the Isle of Raasay. Our accommodation was a two bedroom cottage and was so different from our flat in the middle of the city. Andrew was only about six weeks old when we moved, and so poor Helen was moved to a new church, new, home, new community of people as well as being a new mum in the space of six weeks.

It was difficult, as the church was much more traditional than our previous church but it had a man at the helm who had been saved during the Lewis revival and was a powerful preacher of the gospel.

The Highland Island people were so hospitable and very welcoming, we developed really good friendships in our time at the fellowship. I gained so much from John Ferguson being my mentor, we would often meet for prayer times and planning for what I should be involved in, on a weekly basis. I was aware of a group of people hungry for God and to see the kingdom come in great revival power in Skye. I was preaching about once per week as there was both morning and evening services, and the people were very gracious to this wee lad from Glasgow.

On one occasion John asked me to accompany him to Scorrybreac, at the clan Nicolson memorial to dedicate a new seat. There was going to be the gathering of clan members from USA attending this dedication and I was eager to see how John did a seat dedication. The day before this clan gathering, John contacted me to say that he could not do the dedication as something else had come up, and that I would have to do it. I said,

'How do you dedicate a seat?'

'I am sure the Lord will guide you.'

I had a funny feeling that John was happy to get out of this event and leave it to me. Talk about being thrown in at the deep end! The day arrived and I was still perplexed as to what to say and how to dedicate this seat. I arrived at the clan Nicolson memorial and there were about 50 clan members in their kilts, with bagpipes blaring and this procession all to dedicate a seat! As I looked over to Ben Tianavaig, I drew inspiration from Psalm 121, and said:

"I lift up my eyes to the hills - where does my help come from? My help comes from the Lord the Maker of heaven and earth. As my act of dedication of this seat, may everyone who brings themselves to rest on this seat, find inspiration by looking to the hills to find that our help is not in the hills, but in the one who created them. In Jesus' name. Amen!"

Our first Christmas on Skye was spectacular. On Christmas Eve during the afternoon it started to snow really heavily, and I was to take part in the watchnight service starting at 11.30pm. We ended up snowed in. I could not get my car out as the snow was so thick, so I decided to walk the two miles down into the village for the watchnight service.

I eventually arrived wearing my wellies, and was surprised to see the church packed at 11.30pm.

We had a wonderful Christmas Eve service and then I had to walk the two miles back home, eventually getting into bed about 2am.

I still kept links with my home church in Wester Hailes and I was invited by Mike Dawson the associate minister, and who had been my spiritual mentor for the last few years, to go out to Moldova with him, through the ministry headed up by Iain Campbell, called Messianic Servant Ministries (MSM), an outreach ministry that shared the gospel with Jewish people. It was an honour to be asked. This would be for a period of seven days and we would be visiting local Jewish families in the capital city called Kishinev, where interestingly the first Jewish church had been planted in Europe.

We were invited to go in February; Helen went with Andrew to stay for the week in Wester Hailes with Penny Dawson.

The Sunday before we were to fly out, a

lady came up to me and Mike after the church service and said, 'I believe God has given me a word for you both, but it does not make sense to me.' And she shared it from Ezekiel 3:15: *'I came to the exiles who lived at Tel Abib near the Kebar River. And there, where they were living, I sat among them for seven days – deeply distressed.'* At the time we did not understand the word, but during and after our visit to Moldova we certainly did know the reality of that word, as we did sit with Jewish exiles for a period of seven days and we were overwhelmed!

The next day Mike and I flew out to Budapest, and met up with Iain who accommodated us for the night, before flying the next day to Kishinev. That evening Iain anointed us with oil and prayed for the Holy Spirit to anoint and bless our time in Moldova. Next day we flew into Kishinev and it was freezing, snow everywhere, it was and felt a very depressing place to live in. It was a poor country with massive craters of pot-holes in the roads, cold and uninviting.

We were met by the MSM worker, who we were staying with for the next few days, in a high rise flat in the middle of Kishinev.

Our time was spent predominately being taken to Jewish homes where the majority of the people had lost someone during the

Holocaust, and had survived it themselves, many were living in poverty. We were taken to one home where a grandmother with her two grandchildren were having a Shabbat meal, and they invited us as guests. I was overwhelmed by their poverty and generosity, as they laid this beautiful white cloth on the table, with Sabbath candles, and gave us a feast that they could ill afford. Our gifts to them were chocolate and some items of clothing that the church gave us to take over, and they were so grateful. We had such a blessed Sabbath. We heard story after story of the loss that these precious people had experienced during the Holocaust, and yet they welcomed two Christian ministers into their homes to eat at their table.

We were overwhelmed for the seven days we were there. On the Saturday we were invited to share a few words at their Messianic Sabbath service, and it was incredible to see so many attend and sit in a very cold hall, but the worship was warm, and the Lord Yeshua was present through His Holy Spirit in our gathering.

The next day, Sunday, Mike and I were invited to share at a local Pentecostal church, and it was electric, people were giving their lives to the Lord and were being saved in this former communist country, a great awakening was happening.

I was asked to share, and before I got up to speak through an interpreter, there was a power cut which lasted a few minutes and then the power came on again. God gave me a word to share about the power of the Holy Spirit that never cuts out that we can have if we call on the name of the Lord.

I shared part of my testimony and felt that I was to make another invitation for people to come and receive Christ, after a few moments a woman came forward and gave her life to Jesus. What a glorious moment that was. The Lord has done great things for us and we are filled with joy!

My trip to Moldova was overwhelming and life changing, as it made me see the power of the faith of many of these believers, who had been through so much hardship and poverty, yet they were rich in the Lord!

We returned back to Skye and we started putting into place preparations for a summer mission in Portree. Mike Dawson was coming with a team in the summer to help us with the week-long outreach.

The people in the community were really friendly, and just as well. One beautiful summer's day I was walking past the church building and lots of people were out enjoying the sun, two young guys were in the grounds of the church, lying on the grass enjoying a couple of cans of beer. I picked up the courage to go over and speak to them. I said,

'It is nice you could come into the church grounds and as you are here how about I tell you a wee bit about Jesus,'

They said to my surprise, 'Sure go for it.'

I started to share about Gods love from John 3:16 and we had an amazing study on the lawn in the church grounds. I did not receive any of their beer by the way, but I did leave something of God's love for them to think about!

Our time was coming to an end in Portree but there was one small matter of where next Lord? I had applied for two congregations, one in Carstairs, and the other in South Carntyne, Glasgow. I was interviewed by both vacancy committees and invited to preach at neutral church venues. I had been informed by Carstairs that I was on the short list of candidates, in fact it was between me and another minister, and they would let me know on Monday morning who had been chosen.

Meanwhile I had a phone call from Tom, one of the elders at South Carntyne, saying that they had decided to invite me to preach as sole nominee for the vacancy. I was stunned but was not sure what God was saying in all of this. I thanked Tom and said I would get back to him before Sunday evening. I shared this with Helen, before I was going out to take an afternoon service at Budhmor, a residential home for older people. When I arrived, to my surprise, John Ferguson was there, and I mentioned that I thought he had made a mistake, as I was down to do the service that day. He said,

'That is fine, you can have a day off, sit with the people and I will preach.'

John took the passage from John 10:9: '*I am the door; whoever enters through Me will be saved. He will come in and go out and find pasture.*' He started by saying that, 'a door has been opened for you today, and you have to go through that door! The Lord has opened it for you today!'

I felt the power of the Holy Spirit confirming to me that I was to go to South Carntyne.

I was to go home and phone Tom, and accept their offer to preach as sole nominee in Glasgow. The door is opened today, go through that door. John kept emphasising this! After he had finished preaching and talking with the people, I spoke with him explaining that God had confirmed to me through his message I was to go to South Carntyne. I should also point out that John had no knowledge of my conversation with Tom inviting me to be sole nominee. John very wisely said, 'It wasn't a mistake after all that I should have been here to preach!'

We were excited about the new challenge that lay ahead of us moving to Glasgow, but before we left a dear Christian friend Morag, said to me, 'God will bring you back to live and minister in Portree someday!' It was a wrench to leave Skye, part of my heart stayed in Portree when we moved to Glasgow, and although we believed it was the call of God we cried when we saw the contrast of the place which we were going to call home in Dennistoun, to that we had called home in Skye. Not only were we going to a new home and new ministry, but we were to have a new addition to our family in the months ahead as Helen was expecting our second child.

5: A NEW DAY IS DAWNING - GLASGOW

*Let Glasgow flourish through the preaching
of Thy word and the praising of Thy name!*

I was going back to Glasgow, to my home
town, a place which like many of the
cities in our country, was changing in
terms of new housing and regeneration of
communities that had fallen on hard times.
Carntyne was one of those areas, and was in
the middle of old tenement housing being
pulled down and new houses being put in
place; but it still had many social problems
that were not being dealt with. Drug
addiction, poverty, many on the dole, sexual
immorality, adultery, mental health issues

and the list can go on. Yet at the heart of all these problems are people. They are more than a number on the dole queue or live in a place that does not have the right postcode. All people who need love, hope, forgiveness and peace, and whenever a society or nation take God out of the equation it faces real difficulties.

My Glasgow had dropped the most important part of its motto, used many years before I was born, by leaving the God bit out, and just promoting it as 'Let Glasgow flourish!' When a city or community or nation leaves God out I believe we are heading in a downward spiral. My call to Glasgow for the time I was there, was to put God back into Glasgow in the area and parish in which I served the people of Carntyne, so that it can flourish again through the preaching of His word and the praising of His name. As ministers of the gospel we are to preach the good news of the kingdom of God, and wherever His word is preached and His praise is sung, we will see lives flourish under His blessing.

It was with much gratitude to the Lord and His people, that I was ordained into the Parish of South Carntyne church in September 1996, with all my family and friends there as well as many new friends from Skye. It was a wonderful evening, and I felt very humbled to be given the opportunity to serve God and His people in an area of Glasgow that I was not familiar with. I am from the north of the city and this was the east end.

Carntyne had many problems of social deprivation, poor housing, unemployment, drug and alcohol abuse and many other social issues. Our fellowship was a light in the community involved in café outreaches, youth ministries and older generation ministries. We were a small congregation in a very challenging community, however we were a bible believing, Spirit filled group of believers, who loved the Lord and one another.

When pastoral visiting in Carntyne I had to wear my dog collar, as I was going into areas where there was much drug dealing. I soon got to be accepted as I had my uniform on. I remember on one occasion sitting on the kerb with a wee boy who was on his own and waiting on his mum coming back, he was about eight years old and just wanted to talk with someone and that happened to be me. I missed a presbytery meeting waiting with this wee lad for his mum to come home; there are some things that are more important!

I was preaching twice on a Sunday every

week, leading bible study and prayer meetings. We introduced an Alpha course at the manse and I was involved in a lot of pastoral visitation of the congregation to get to know the people.

We were having our first Christmas in Dennistoun and had many Christmas services to prepare for. I was looking forward to taking my first Christmas Eve watchnight service at Carntyne, starting at 11.30pm. It was a very special evening as many people came into the building, people I had never seen before. After the service I was shaking hands with the people and wishing them a happy Christmas, there was one guy I spoke to and asked if he was visiting family and he said, 'I will have you know minister, this is my church, I come here every year on Christmas Eve!' That was me told!

Not only was it great excitement for Andrew to have his first Christmas in Glasgow celebrating the birth of Jesus, but another baby was due to be born and our daughter Sarah was born, Saturday evening on the 4th January 1997 at Rutherglen Maternity Hospital. Like our first born this was of great joy to us and we were thrilled at welcoming Sarah Elizabeth into our family.

In those days there was no paternity leave and I left the hospital at midnight to head home to prepare myself for Sunday morning worship.

I got up first thing in the morning to collect Andrew from my mum's to take him to see his new baby sister, before we went on to church. It was a busy and tiring time but we were so grateful to the Lord for blessing us with two beautiful children.

It was Pentecost Sunday and I had just finished preaching on the fire of the Holy Spirit, during the worship I was asking the Lord if we could make some impact on the many people in our community who never came to church. As I was about to leave the church and was walking towards my car, I saw a group of about six teenage lads around my car, one sitting on top of it. I prayed,

'Lord, what will I do?' As I approached these lads one of them turned to me and said,

'Hey, I know you? You did my grannie's funeral, and I have been finding things hard going!'

God had opened a door for me to speak with these guys, I tried to comfort the young lad and give him some hope. I asked them,

'What can the church do for you?'

'Gies a joab!' (give us a job)

'I would love to give you a job but I don't have any, but is there anything you like to do?'

'Aye, play fitba!'

'Ok' I said, 'Let's start a football team.' And they thought this would be great!

We started the following Wednesday and hired the local catholic high school hall and started a weekly training session. We ended up with about 15 guys turning up every week, so we decided to enter the evangelical churches league, the rules being that you had to have at least three Christians playing in the team. I was the only Christian as all the lads were not Christians. Praise the Lord, a guy whose wife was a big part of our church, got converted in a wonderful way, during a football outreach that Iain Cameron ran every week in Scotstoun, where we would play seven-a-side football. At least half of us were Christians, and we invited non-Christians to play and then go for a drink with them afterwards.

On one occasion, this guy Sandy, who had been getting convicted by the Lord during the time he had been going along to my church with his wife, but kept trying to run away from committing his life to Jesus.

Later after his conversion I asked him,

'How did it happen?'

'It was after football one night I joined you all for a drink and I noticed that one of you Christian guys had a pint of beer, I had thought for me to become a Christian I would have to give up everything, before God would accept me. It dawned on me, it is what Jesus Christ has done for me in his love on the cross, and in my turning to him that I am saved, and I don't need to give up having a pint now and again unless God leads me to do so.'

Sandy's life was changed and he became a leader within our church. God had also given Sandy to us as a footballer, so that we could run this football team for our local community. He also had a friend who was a Christian and footballer from another church and wanted to get involved in this outreach to these young men. Praise the Lord! I now had three Christians, including myself and we were accepted into the league.

We managed, along with the lads, to raise money for our new strips, and South Carntyne Team was formed in 1997, in time for the beginning of the new season in September.

Our first match was away from home, and I was a bit uncertain how these young guys would cope in this adult Christian league especially in the discipline side of things. Some of these lads were notorious for fighting and losing their temper, and as a team we were trying to instil in them some ways of dealing with their temper. We arrived at our first game and we were getting ready in the changing room and after my team talk I asked:

'Lads do you mind if I pray? If you feel you don't need it I certainly do!'

'Aye no problem, go for it,' some of them said.

I prayed for us to have a good game and for control and protection from injuries or injuring another, in Jesus' name, Amen! We did well for our first game and we had an encouraging 2-2 draw.

Over the weeks we did not do too well, we had been losing and some lads losing their heads. One particular Saturday morning I woke up early, and felt that the Lord was prompting me to pray for the lads before the start of the next game.

We were to play a team from the Glasgow Bible College who were a very good and strong team, and as I was getting this prompting from the Lord I felt he was saying, 'and pray that they will win!'

We arrived at Carntyne Park to play this game and as we went into get changed a young lad from the team said to me,

'Minister you have not been praying for us before the start of a game and I think that is why we are not doing so well.'

I replied, 'God told me that I should pray for you all today.'

'Do it then!'

I started to pray and as I was doing so a battle was going on in my mind, as I felt I was being told to pray for a victory, but the other side of me was thinking, we have no chance against this team and if you pray for a win and we don't win, you won't look so good. What a battle. I surrendered to the still voice of calm and challenge and I prayed, 'Heavenly Father, I pray that you give us a victory today, in Jesus' name, Amen!'

We won 7-3 that day, and as we came into the dressing room after the game, you could hear a pin drop, and the young guy who asked for me to pray stood up and said, 'I told you so, God answers prayer.'

You can have all your theological doctrines and arguments about prayer and how God does or does not answer prayer, but on that day for that one young man and a young team and the management team and the minister from South Carntyne, God indeed answered our prayer. To God be the glory!

Things started to change in our church, some people were being saved and getting filled with the Holy Spirit, the football team was going well, in fact the boys of the team protected the church building from vandalism as we would often get break-ins or broken windows in the past. One lad said, 'This is my church and nobody will do anything to the building,' and nobody did.

I wanted the very best for the people of Carntyne, and wanted to have a building and a café that would be something beautiful for the Lord, a place of solace and welcoming to the community.

Our hall where we had run the café was dark and depressing, although the people were light and love.

Our vision was for restoration, and we developed a relationship with Tearfund UK Action, who helped finance church projects amongst the poorer communities in the UK. We were successful in becoming a partner with them, and our co-ordinator for helping us implement the project was David Greaves, who lived in London, and was a pastor of a predominately black church in London.

We were awarded a grant of £10,000 to redevelop our halls, and we put in new floors, ceilings, and a kitchen and redecorated our halls. Some of the ladies of the church made beautiful wall banners, based on Psalm 23, the Lord is my shepherd. The café was beautiful and a place of peace, a solace in a busy urban area, which offered ministry to both body, mind, spirit and stomachs!

Our large hall was renovated and we developed a Christian nursery for the young children in the area; we ran summer clubs, started a J-Team club, and our fellowship was thriving, not just surviving.

We were further blessed by Scripture Union who wanted to employ a youth worker in the Carntyne area to work in the schools and alongside our church, we were blessed to have Libby Lobban appointed to work alongside our team.

Many amazing things were happening but within my spirit I was not completely settled, I missed Skye and the people, my time in Portree had changed me and drawn me to an island ministry hopefully in the future.

Helen and I were delighted to announce to our family and the church that she was expecting again, we were thrilled that God was blessing us with another baby.

Andrew and Sarah were developing well and seemed to be enjoying their time in Glasgow, especially seeing granny and granda about twice a week, where they were truly spoiled by my parents' generosity. It was a great blessing and help that my mum and dad could look after the children at times.

My mum Isabel, and dad George, started

to attend Carntyne church and were regulars.

My mum was converted in 1957 at a Billy Graham rally in the Kelvin Hall in Glasgow, and according to my dad he had been a choir boy at St Matthew's Church in Possilpark, as a youngster.

My mum never had good health, and almost lost her life when I was about 12 years old. She never really got over the major operation and illness she had; she learnt to live with much pain and discomfort but was always a help and a blessing to us. My dad on the other hand was pretty healthy, but suffered great trauma during his time on National Service with the Highland Light Infantry in Cyprus. He witnessed and lost many of his friends when a booby trap bomb went off at a well, as the soldiers went to get a drink, killing many of them. My dad to this day finds it hard to understand, but is very thankful that his life was spared. Some people live with a lot of trauma in their life and find it hard to talk about it and some turn to alcohol to drown their sorrows. Later on in his life my dad would turn to Jesus, and experience the peace of God that passes all understanding, touching his life.

Completely out of the blue, I started training for the Nazareth Bike ride which was to take place in Israel during November of 1998, I can't quite remember how I got involved with this. I must have been reading the Edinburgh Medical Missionary Society's newsletter and noticed that they were trying to raise funds for the Nazareth Hospital, which is a Christian medical centre in the heart of Nazareth. As I have a love for the Jewish people and the Land, I thought it might be a worthwhile thing to do. I prayed about it and I did not hear God say that I should not do it. In fact, my dear Helen thought it was a good thing to do, even though we had two very young children and another on the way. I had not been on a bike for years, and the bike ride would be covering a distance of 250 miles in five days. Now for a cyclist that is no big deal, but for someone who had no bike, and it was now June and I hadn't raised any money, the minimum to raise was £2,500, I felt a bit out of my depth. Yet I felt this inner prompting to register for it, so I did and was accepted. I managed to borrow a bike which was in a poor condition and not the right size, and boy, what a struggle that was.

Yet God had other people to help me out. Two significant things happened. First, was a lady from my church came to me and said you are not to worry about raising the

£2,500, God has given me the money to give to you! Wow! Praise the Lord! Second, I contacted the local police to ask if they had any bikes that they were selling that had not been claimed. The officer asked what I needed it for, and to cut a long story short, the police got together and bought me a brand new bike and presented it to me, with a photographer from the local newspaper taking photos and getting my story.

This story attracted much local attention and was a good witness for the gospel and our local church. It also helped to raise a lot more money for the Nazareth Hospital, by the time I left for the ride in November, through the generosity of a community of people who were not well off, I had raised £4,500. I only had the little matter of doing a 250 mile bike ride, which was around the north of the country, from Mount Carmel up towards Mount Hermon, down to the Sea of Galilee then heading up to Nazareth.

What an experience that was, as we were arriving at the finishing line at the Nazareth Hospital, the town came to a standstill, as 100 cyclists in their yellow jerseys were welcomed into the town, with the bagpipes playing and people cheering at our arrival. It was very humbling, and after seeing the hospital and meeting staff and patients, it confirmed to us that it was a blessing to the community and to us, we had raised up to a £100,000 for the important medical and gospel work in the place where Jesus grew up.

It was March 1999 that our third child, Rachel Helen, was born in Glasgow Southern General at the weekend of our churches communion, and I had invited a guest preacher from Plockton Free Church, Rev Roddie Rankin to preach. We had Roddy stay at the manse for the weekend, as it was on the Friday that Helen was taken into hospital, and poor Roddie had to put up with my cooking for the weekend, which included everything made from tins, beef stew, beans, potatoes, peas. Roddy was a great blessing and put up with my dreadful cooking. I don't think he has ever gotten over that culinary experience!

Rachel was born on the 12th March 1999, and I remember taking Andrew and Sarah to see their new wee sister. Sarah took baby Rachel in her arms and started to cuddle her with tears in her eyes, and Andrew was giving his mum a big cuddle. We were abundantly blessed by the Lord, now having three beautiful children. '*Sons are a heritage from the Lord, children a reward from him.*' (Psa. 127:3).

It was going really well in church and in our family life. Yes! It was busy and quite stressful being the minister of the parish, and having a baby and two toddlers. Helen had felt it was her calling to be a mother at home, looking after the children and bringing them up. For me, that is a high calling and one that Helen did amazingly well. I actually marvel at the patience and joy she showed through those challenging and exhausting times. I was still experiencing a restlessness within the ministry in Carntyne and living in Glasgow; I could not get Skye and its people out of my mind and heart, and about a year later I had a telephone call that took me by surprise.

John Ferguson had called, asking me to come over to Skye to help with sharing the gospel. John was the interim moderator of the newly extended parish of Bracadale and Duirinish, in north-west Skye. He quoted from Acts 16: 9-10: *'During the night Paul had a vision of a man of Macedonia standing and begging him, "Come over to Macedonia and help us." After Paul had seen the vision, we got ready at once to leave for Macedonia, concluding that God had called us to preach the gospel to them.'* John asked me to prayerfully consider coming back to Skye to help with the sharing of the gospel in this newly formed united parish that extended from Dunvegan, Waternish, Glendale all the way south to Struan, Carbost and Portnalong. I told John that I would give it much prayer and thought and get back to him in due course.

When I put the phone down I felt a real excitement spring up within me, similar to that when I was first called to Carntyne, over three years ago, this man John Ferguson had been instrumental in my call to leave Skye and head to Glasgow, now this same man was being used again by God to prompt me to leave Glasgow and go back to Skye.

In my excitement I shared this news with Helen, but she was not as enthusiastic as me and with good reason. She reminded me that we had only been in Glasgow for just over three years and were just settling in, what about the people? What about your mum and dad? I said, 'Let's not dismiss it, it might be the Lord is calling us to go, let us pray and share about it in the next few weeks.'

I loved the people that the Lord had called me to in Glasgow, and I was in a very privileged position to have shared in their lives, both highs and lows over the past few years, was it right to leave now? I still had this desire and excitement in my soul to pursue this call for help to the next level, and I would be heading up to Portree on a Sunday morning to preach at the church where the vacancy committee would be in attendance. After I finished the service I said the usual goodbyes and headed back to Glasgow. I felt a peace about it and prayed, 'Not my will but your will be done, Lord. If this is you calling me to go to Skye please make it clear one way or another.'

A few days later I got an invitation to preach as sole nominee for the vacant parish, and along with Helen and my children we were to go at a convenient time. I was bubbling with joy, but the reality of it all hit me, that if I go I am leaving Glasgow for good, my church, my home, my people, my parents. Three major hurdles to overcome; first, I had only been in my first charge for three and a half years and there was an unwritten rule you were to be there for five years. Second, how would my mum and dad feel about me taking their grandchildren all the way to Skye. Third, our partnership as a church with Tearfund UK Action.

We travelled in faith to Skye one weekend to see around Dunvegan, the manse, parish and to preach. It was incredible to be at the church building in Dunvegan, where we had planned the date of our wedding nine years previously. Helen and I talked a lot about what to do. I think I was more convinced at the time, of us being called. So we left it with the Lord, and that we would have peace about the decisions that we would make together in the coming days.

I preached on the Sunday morning at Dunvegan Church of Scotland, and after the service the congregation had a vote and they unanimously voted to invite me to be their new minister.

We felt that this was a major door that God was opening up to us, in conformation of our call. I thanked the vacancy committee and said that I would have to go back to Glasgow presbytery, and my own congregation, to inform them.

When we got back to Glasgow I called a kirk session meeting to let them know that I had been called to be new minister on Skye, and that I believed that this was the Lord's will. To my surprise no one objected, my session clerk said: 'We will miss you, but if it is the Lord's calling you have to go.'

I then had to make a special appeal to presbytery and I remember the presbytery clerk saying to me,

'Are you wanting to leave because you have fallen out with people?'

I was stunned at his question and said, 'No I love these people and have not fallen out with anyone, and if I had, does this constitute a call to leave a congregation? No, I believe God is calling us to go!' He presented the call to presbytery and without a complaint or any negative comments presbytery approved the call. First major hurdle crossed!

I now had to go and share this news with my parents, and felt this would be the hardest of all. I plucked up the courage to tell them and there were many tears, but my mum said, 'I always felt you would go back to Skye.' This was the hardest thing for me to do.

My third hurdle was our partnership with Tearfund, and our project manager David Greaves was due to pay us a visit. He was coming to the manse and he pulled up in his car and I noticed that he did not come in right away. He eventually came to the door and I invited him in. I said,

'David, I have something to tell you.'

'I know, you are leaving South Carntyne to go to another church.'

'How did you know this?'

'God has just told me in my car, and I believe that it is a call for you to go!'

I was awe struck. This for me was the

confirmation that I needed from the Lord that I was doing was the right thing. God had dealt with my three major hurdles by getting me over them, and preparing the way ahead for Helen and my children to make another new journey back to the land, culture and a people that I had come to love.

6: A NEW MILLENIUM, AND NEW PASTURES: SKYE

We left Glasgow giving thanks to God for our time there, the Lord had blessed us with the additions of Sarah and Rachel to our family and along with Andrew we left with many tears but also with much excitement for the challenge ahead.

We arrived at Duirinish Manse at the beginning of July in 2000, the air smelled sweet and the location of the manse was awesome. I remember saying to the Lord I will really need to hear you speak to me if I am ever to leave this place because I could spend the rest of my life here. The manse had a massive garden space, and even bigger glebe, which one of the biggest in the Highlands, it was modern and the children each had their own room. God gave us so many good memories of that house and village that every time I go back there I feel as if it is home.

For the next six years it was to be our home, and I was inducted into the ministry of Bracadale and Duirinish parish. The induction was humbling and the Highland hospitality was overwhelming.

It was like a wedding reception with the top table reserved for my family, as well as the leaders of the church. The food was plentiful and the speeches were encouraging, but the one thing I will never forget as we neared the end of the evening was an elder got up to sing Psalm 72:17-19:

'His name forever shall endure, last like the sun it shall, men shall be blessed in Him are blessed all nations shall him call. And blessed be the Lord our God, the God of Israel, for He alone doth wondrous works, in glory that excel. And blessed be His glorious name to all eternity; the whole earth let his glory fill. Amen, so let it be.'

What a way to end the induction and to begin a new ministry which our fellowship would have together, where we would see the gospel impacting many in our community in the months and years ahead.

The Parish of Bracadale and Duirinish was newly formed after the ministers Rory Macleod of Bracadale, and Mike Lind of Duirinish, went on to new pastures.

It covered many miles and had in the past five places of worship at Dunvegan, Waternish, Glendale, Carbost and Portnalong.

The two main centres of worship were now in the villages of Dunvegan and Carbost.

It was a very challenging parish in as much as the miles it covered trying to look after the flock, as well as reaching into the communities with the gospel.

My six years at the parish were mixed with many challenges from within the congregation, some who did not like to see change and were holding onto the past. Yet there were a godly group of praying people who wanted to see the presence of God move in our communities.

The thing that I was not really prepared for, was funerals. During my time in Glasgow most were at the crematorium and lasted no more than 20 minutes, but in this parish it was and still is, a community event wherein at my first funeral it seemed that all of Skye had attended, and it lasted for hours.

There was something really powerful

about this that people gathered to support and encourage the grieving families. I realised that it was also a way of bringing the gospel into a community of people, many who were not believers or only nominal church goers, by offering them the hope of eternal life in Jesus.

Hope beyond the grave! An endless hope not a hopeless end! I was learning that my gifting from the Lord was one of an evangelist, and I felt I could share the word in a way that could get people to think about their lives with, or without Christ.

Doors started to open in the communities for a schools ministry. I was invited to be part of the chaplaincy team for Dunvegan, Waternish, Glendale, Struan, and Carbost Primary Schools as well as Portree High School. As I walked around the parish or drove around and met many people, God showed me that there was nothing in the villages for boys. We had Guides and Brownies for the girls, but nothing for boys, bearing in mind in those days there were over 70 pupils in Dunvegan School alone!

I thought back to an organisation that had had a big impact on me when I was a boy, the Boys' Brigade, and explored the possibility of starting a company in Dunvegan.

Many in the fellowship caught the vision as well as parents in the community and we started the 1st Bracadale and Duirinish Junior section of the Boys' Brigade.

Through this ministry many families came to the family church services, which I introduced at both churches. On occasions at Carbost I remember the church being packed with people and one wee lad asking where the toilet was. The Carbost church had no toilet other than a bush out in the field!

There was an excitement about the place as new families came into the fellowship, and a few people gave their lives to Jesus. On one occasion, I baptised a whole family of six including the grandmother, who when I first came to the parish said that she would never go to church again, because she was taught as a child and young adult that, all she was destined for was hell fire and damnation. That is what she felt she heard every week and she said, 'What is the point of going to church if there is no hope for me?'

I asked her if she had heard of the gospel of love. '*For God so loved the world that he gave his only begotten son that whosoever believes in him should not perish but have everlasting life.*' (Jn. 3:16). She could not remember hearing that message. We started an Alpha course, to which she came along and gave her life to Jesus, and became a strong member in our fellowship.

In fact, the Alpha course made a massive impact in Dunvegan, for this same lady who owned the Dunvegan Hotel invited us to hold the course there. We did, and sent out invitations, we had over 40 people attend the course. It was awesome! There was an excitement in the air, with spiritual awakening in many people's lives.

There were also challenging faith moments and sadness in the Island, as my daughter Sarah's best friend at nursery died tragically at the age of two. I will never forget the funeral; it still impacts me to this day, the out-pouring of grief that hit this young family and the whole community. The big question in everyone's mind: Why? I felt very confused and I had no answer to that question and to this day I still don't.

There are many highs and lows in parish ministry, many unanswered questions and challenges in life and faith and I will never give any trite answers because I don't have any.

I still trust in God even when I do not know what is happening or why things happen and why storms come to all of us at some time or another.

I take consolation in that the Jesus I

follow went through storms, and his disciples went through storms even when Jesus was with them.

There is the story in Mark 4 when everything was calm and peaceful as Jesus and his disciples set out on a boat journey on the Sea of Galilee to get some rest and peace. As they travelled and completely unexpected a storm hits them, a violent storm. Meanwhile Jesus is sleeping on a cushion, while the disciples are in fear and desperation that the storm is going to end their lives. They cry out to Jesus;

'Teacher, don't you care if we drown?' He got up, rebuked the wind and said to the waves, 'Peace, be still!'

Yes, Jesus cares if we drown. Yes, Jesus is in the boat with us, in the storms of life. Yes, He brings peace into the storms that we face if we call on Him. We may well be Christians but it does not mean that we are immune to facing the storms of this life. I would rather have Jesus in the boat with me than not!

My faith is in Jesus who went through the darkest and most severe storm imaginable, when He faced the cross.

He who did no wrong suffered at the hands of sinful men, He who loved the broken, the confused, the sinner, the imprisoned, the poor, He faced the wrath of evil and wickedness in His love for humanity. The storm died down when he cried from his lips: 'It is finished!' The Hebrew meaning for this phrase, shalom, completeness, wholeness, wellbeing. The words, '*It is finished!*' Broke the wrath of the enemy of death and the devil so much that the apostle Paul wrote, '*Death has been swallowed up in victory. Where, O death, is your victory? Where, O death, is your sting? The sting of death is sin, and the power of sin is the law. But thanks be to God! He gives us the victory through our Lord Jesus Christ.*'(1 Cor. 15:54-56).

Dunvegan Amateur Football Club

I was invited to Dunvegan football club to be involved in playing for the team, and as the new minister in the parish this seemed quite strange to many of the lads, and even the supporters in the community that a minister could play football. I remember my first game was against Sleat and Strath at the primary school park in Dunvegan.

I had not anticipated that there would be such a big crowd gathering to support their local village team. As I was about to enter the dressing room I heard the manager have a stern talk to the lads and the gist of it was:

'We have the minister playing today, so I want you to keep the swearing down.'

Then I walk in and say, 'Hi lads my name is Gary and I am here to play football, be yourselves and let's get on with it.'

I was so glad to play in that team and was blessed to have scored two goals in my debut game, even though we lost. It was a good way to break the ice and get accepted into the football community, which would open doors into young men's lives who never came to church. I was involved in coaching youngsters in the community in football and this gave us the opportunity, for us to start the Boys' Brigade ministry in the village. It was a wonderful time as we were working closely with other churches in the area, from the Free Church, Associated Presbyterian Church, Skye Bible Church who all took part in the youth outreach in the area.

The First Bracadale and Duirinish junior section company was formed and we reached many boys with the gospel over a period of five years or so.

The object of the Boys' Brigade is: The advancement of Christ's kingdom among boys.

We met every week with these lads sharing the gospel in practical and spiritual ways, the company began to grow and we had about 50 boys on the roll. We would take them on trips and one of the highlights was going on a joint outing with the Brownies and Guides, where we took a coach load of young people to Dingwall to meet with Brian Irvine, who played for Ross County at the time and had played for Aberdeen and Scotland throughout his career. Brian was a Christian and he very kindly invited our group for a day out to see Ross County on the last day of their season for free, we had 80 tickets generously donated by Brian, and Roy McGregor the chairman, to bless and encourage our ministry to these young people.

A few months later I invited Brian to come and speak at Dunvegan on a Sunday morning and we decided as a church to have the meeting in the village hall.

It was incredible the car park was full and the hall was bursting to capacity as Brian shared some of his football stories and powerful testimony. I remember as he was coming to end of his talk he said,

' I have Scotland caps and a winning Scottish cup medal and these were great moments in my life, but I notice that the caps are wearing away and the medal is tarnished and will not last for ever. But the greatest thing that happened to me in my life is when I gave my life to Jesus Christ as my saviour and Lord, knowing that He gave his life for me to take away my sin. It was in receiving Jesus Christ into my life that I received the greatest gift of all. Unlike the caps and medals that fade away and don't last forever, my relationship with God through Jesus Christ does last forever!'

It was electric, you could hear a pin drop in a hall that was full of people of all ages. The seed had been sown into many hearts, and I was so thankful to the Lord for being part of the same family of Jesus Christ, that my brother Brian belongs to.

This was not a one off event, over the years Brian visited us many times and gave football and spiritual coaching to many of our young people over the years, and is still a very precious friend to this day.

2005: A special year

Six-week pulpit exchange to North Carolina from July to August with the Amity Presbyterian Church in Charlotte. Rev Bill Yeomans came to Dunvegan with his family, and the five of us went to Charlotte for this exchange. North Carolina has a big Scottish and Irish influence in their history, with many from Scotland immigrating back in the

1800s.

Everywhere we went and when people heard our accent they would be so warm and welcoming. I remember being in a restaurant and ordering food and the waitress asked if I was from Scotland, I responded,

'Yes'

'We love the Scots can I give you a hug?'

'As long as it is alright with my wife.'

The congregation of Amity were a very warm, generous and encouraging fellowship and we made many friends that we keep in touch with today.

I visited a few different churches in my time in Charlotte which was a city congregation. On one occasion I visited a minister who was the pastor of the first Presbyterian Church in Charlotte with a membership of 3,000 people, in the church building they had about seven offices, with a pastor for just about everything: worship, youth, elderly, pastoral care, senior pastor, assistant pastor and the offices went on. It also had a gym and the huge worship area. After all it was the Bible belt that I was in, so when you went to a store like Walmart or Asda, there was a whole section in the supermarket for Christian music, bibles, devotional books, it was the best supermarket experience I have ever had and

I could have stayed in there for hours.

My second Sunday at Amity had been advertised in the local newspaper; 'Isle of Skye Pastor Gary Wilson visits Amity church this coming Sunday, all welcome!'

Many came to church that Sunday more than the previous week, a guy even came with a kilt on and in full Highland regalia.

After the service he came to chat with me, he said, 'I am a Wilson, can you tell me anything about the clan?'

I did not have a clue only that we were from Caithness in the Highlands. I think he might have been a bit disappointed when I also said that I was from Glasgow!

Our six weeks came to an end, we all had a ball, I had even been invited to apply to be a minister in Charlotte but I felt my calling was very strong to be on the Isle of Skye. On my last Sunday an older gentleman came up to me and said, 'Pastor, I have loved having you with us it has been so good, the only problem was that I could not understand a word you said.'

I thought to myself, 'What was the point!'

We had a great send off and were sorry to leave many dear folks but were looking forward to getting back to Skye.

We had been in the parish for five years now and things were going really well.

I had a vision to have an outdoor Christian music outreach event in a field in Dunvegan and I thought it would be good to have some sort of big tent or marquee erected and invite Matt Redman to come and do a weekend event of praise and worship.

I emailed Matt, whom I have never met before, inviting him to Skye and he kindly got back to me saying that he was very thankful for the invitation but would not be able to take up the offer. I was disappointed in as much as I thought I had got the vision wrong.

However about a week later I was preaching at Dunvegan Church and after the service a visitor from America asked to speak with me, she said, 'Pastor, God has given me a word/picture, I see a big tent in the middle of the village and it is going to be a gospel outreach in the heart of the village.'

I thanked her for sharing this with me telling her that I had had a similar word. A few days later I had a phone call from a man called Neil Boddy from Perth Christian Centre, I had never heard of this man before, or ever heard of Perth Christian Centre, and he said,

'Pastor, how would you feel about People With A Mission Ministries (PWAMM) coming to Dunvegan to work with the local churches to have a tent mission?' I was stunned!

'What, you have a big tent?'

'Yes, and we have a mission team to come and be part of it.'

'How much will it cost us?'

'Nothing, other than the churches getting involved together!'

'Hallelujah!' I said, and shared with him the vision I had been given by the Lord!

We prayed, prepared and proclaimed throughout the island about the mission which had been set for summer 2006. There was great unity between the churches in the community and the local community offered accommodation for the team from Perth which numbered about 30 people. We had a children's outreach in the mornings, a family service every evening of that week and a wonderful OAP event by bringing all our elderly folk into the tent, giving them an amazing afternoon tea and the gospel.

The place was buzzing.

Every evening meeting the power of the Holy Spirit was in that tent, people's lives were being touched they were being born again and saved, people from all over the island came to Dunvegan for that week in July.

A glorious week indeed. I was inundated with people wanting to be baptized in Loch

Dunvegan and we must have had between 15-20 full immersions that week.

I have never experienced such a move of the Holy Spirit and people's lives being changed. God was doing a work in children, adults and the elderly. It was as in the days of Pentecost:

'In the last days, God says, I will pour out my Spirit on all people. Your sons and daughters will prophesy, your young men will see visions, your old men will dream dreams. Even on my servants, both men and women, I will pour out my Spirit in those days, and they will prophesy... And everyone who calls on the name of the Lord will be saved.' (Acts 2:17-21).

7: A NEW CALL – PORTREE

During this time, I was feeling quite down by the direction that the Church of Scotland were taking, going more and more away from the authority of the word of God in its practice. Unbiblical and heretical teachings were coming in through liberals who held many of the offices of power in the boards and structures of the national church, whereas the more evangelical and Spirit-filled men and women were out serving in front line parish ministry. Many bible believing ministers were very troubled by what was coming into the church and over the next few years many, sadly would leave their parishes.

I had built up a good relationship with

Pastor Alistair Matheson of Skye Bible Church (SBC) over the past six years, we worked on joint services and outreaches together. I called Alistair one day asking for some advice about the Pentecostal church. He asked,

'Why?'

'I feel that I might be being led away from the Church of Scotland as over the years I have felt like a Pentecostal in a Presbyterian church.' He listened to me for a while, then he said words that I could not quite take in,

'Why don't you become pastor of Skye Bible Church?'

'Quite simply because you are the pastor.'

'We are looking for a full time pastor.'

At the time Alistair was a high school teacher in Portree and was doing the pastor role as well as a full time job. I was taken aback! Was this the voice of God prompting me through this brother? What would Helen make of it? We chatted and prayed about it. I felt a prompting in my spirit, but I loved the people of Bracadale and Duirinish, I loved living in Dunvegan, I loved the manse where we lived. But I was reminded of what I said to the Lord when I first arrived in Dunvegan, that He would need to make it clear to me when it was time for me to go, as I could be here for the rest of my life. Well

God was making it clear and challenging me to trust Him.

I met with Alistair Matheson every Monday over a period of six weeks at 7.00am in the morning, for prayer together, and it was becoming increasingly moving in my spirit that the Lord was in this and that He was leading us to new pastures.

I was invited by Samuel McKibben and Alistair to go to their National Apostolic Church conference in Swansea, where I spent three or four days with these men of God. At the conference God spoke to me very clearly through the national leader, Warren Jones, who did not know me, but was speaking to the gathering of people which would have been around 1000, and he looked over in my direction in the crowd and he started prophesying these words:

'You are going to be uprooted and replanted and you are wondering if this is the right thing to do. Trust in God and He will uproot you and replant you. It's time to do it!'

I was zapped by the power of the Holy Spirit, I was convicted that the word was for me and my family. I could hardly take it in it was awesome!

After the meeting, I was walking out of

the venue and who should I bump into, none other than Warren Jones. I said to him about the word he had shared and how I felt that God had spoken it into my life, but I also said that it could have been for anyone in the congregation. He stunned me by saying,

'No it was for you!'

'How can you be sure?'

'Because no one else has come and shared with me what you have.'

Wow! On a few occasions later over the years, Warren would not only speak the word of God prophetically into my life but also into the life of SBC. I had to phone Helen and let her know that God had spoken to me, and she was in agreement. When I returned Helen and I both knew that the Lord had spoken to us, *'This is the way walk you in it.'* (Isa. 30:21).

The day arrived when I had to inform my congregation that SBC had called me to be their pastor, and it was a sad and emotionally draining time for me. I loved the people of the parish and to say that I was leaving, felt as if I was letting people down, but I believed that the Lord had spoken and it was time to move on.

I was to leave the manse in October, the church had been very kind to let me stay on until then.

The big challenge was that I had a wife and three children to support, and to find a home for us, as we would have to give up our beautiful home where we had lived for the past six years. Helen and I went to consult a mortgage advisor and he put it very realistically to us, that we would not be able to get much of a mortgage, and we would be struggling to get a house with two bedrooms, far less than the three we were looking for. My income was going to be considerably reduced when leaving the Church of Scotland and we had also had a home which we did not have to pay for. We left that meeting very down and dejected, and the thought came to me as to whether I was doing the right thing. We put our name down on the housing list, and again it was not looking good.

In the short term we had to find accommodation for October, which was only one month away. Friends from America contacted us out of the blue, offering us their beautiful house in Colbost for four months, which we readily accepted.

Over the next few weeks we settled into our temporary home, and our new congregation, who let me preach, visit and get to know them all before my induction as pastor, the date had been set for the first week in February 2007. We were looking for and praying for God to open a door, quite literally, for a permanent home before February. Things were quite tight financially but God was providing for us every step of the way. During my quiet time one morning, God gave me a song of encouragement. I have never been inspired to write a song but the Lord in his graciousness gave me this one that has blessed and encouraged me right up to this day. The following words came to me:

I have a song in my heart for Yahweh Yireh! He is my great provider each and every-day.

I have a song in my heart for Yahweh Yireh! He is my great provider each and every-day.

I live to praise his wonderful name! I live to praise his glorious name!

I live to praise the name above names, Hallelujah! What a Saviour glory to his name.

Yahweh Yireh is the Hebrew phrase meaning 'God Provides' and over the next few months and years He always did, and has always provided for us as a family. A door was opened for us to have our first mortgaged house in Portree, quite miraculously. We went to visit a house in

Stormyhill Terrace, it had three bedrooms and an asking price too high for us, but I made the owners an offer on the basis that we would get a mortgage, and they accepted it. It was a big step of faith as I did not have the asking price, in fact I did not have anything. The word was given to me by Alistair Matheson one night: *'My God will supply all of your needs according to His glorious riches in Christ Jesus.'* (Phil. 4:19). God will make a way where there seems to be no way!

Praise the Lord, we were offered a mortgage but it fell way short of what we needed, and someone encouraged us to apply for a grant from the Scottish Housing Association, they were giving grants to first time buyers who were going to live and work in the community for the next 10 years.

We met all the criteria and were awarded a wonderful amount of grant that covered the short fall of the mortgage loan, and we would not have to pay it back unless we sold the house before the 10 year period ended. I have a song in my heart for Yahweh Yireh, He is my great provider each and every day! We moved into our new house at the end of January 2007 just before my ordination.

I want to thank my wife Helen, and my children Andrew, Sarah and Rachel who all put up with very challenging and unsettling times as they moved away from the Dunvegan area to Portree. I was ordained and inducted as pastor of SBC at a wonderful celebration service in Portree Community Centre, where hundreds gathered to welcome me and my family into the new role, it was so pleasing to see many of my previous congregation gathering at this act of worship.

Starting within a new denomination certainly had its challenges, which I never anticipated. There was a very strong leadership team, who had been leaders longer than I had been a pastor and I found it difficult to adjust to their style of eldership.

I had a lot of learning to do and a lot of humility to show towards my fellow leaders. I enjoyed the freedom in worship and the praise, prayer and preaching of the word was inspirational. The great thing was that it was a young and vibrant church and a few months into my role I was asked to take over leadership of the Youth Group, something I had never really felt comfortable with, I prayed to the Lord and He reassured me that this was the right move and to fully commit myself to the young people.

This youth ministry was a blessing as we

had many gifted young people who were Christians, on fire for the Lord, and who sang and played musical instruments. Many young people were coming to faith and being baptised, it was a purple patch in the ministry among the teenagers. We went to Christian youth events in Inverness and Edinburgh. We did a mission in Bothwell for a week along with Dave Brackenridge and everything was going well and really exciting.

However, our lives were about to be challenged as we as a family went through a time of uncertainty and pain. Helen had been diagnosed with breast cancer which floored all of us.

It was the hardest moment of my life.

I had been with Helen to Raigmore Breast Unit to get her examination results and as she was in seeing the consultant, I felt that the Lord gave me a word from Jeremiah 29:11, *"For I know the plans I have for you," declares the Lord, "plans to prosper you and not to harm you, plans to give you hope and a future."* I thought she probably does not have cancer, it will be fine. Helen came out from the meeting asking me to go back in and see the consultant who said, 'I am sorry to say that it is cancer.'

I felt sick, I felt our world was falling

apart. I felt that I could not do anything, I was done in. I thought so much for that word from God... plans to prosper you and not to harm you... Is that the way you show it God? I must have heard wrong! I must confess I was holding on to God by the skin of my teeth. I was afraid. How can this happen to us Lord?

The consultant tried to give us hope and reassurance that it was a small tumour and was not aggressive, and that Helen would require a lumpectomy followed by radiotherapy. It was a very good prognosis!

However, I felt so low and afraid and to be honest with you so upset with God. I don't know how I managed to preach some of those Sundays leading up to Helen's operation, I had barely any faith left. Yet, on one occasion, Alistair spoke prophetically to both of us, he looked us in the eye and said,

'All will be well.' He kept saying it over and over again! It was reassuring, but did I trust that all would be well?

One thing about cancer is that it leaves you numb, it does bring fear to you and your family, so many tests, so many results to wait for, you are always on edge, which is why you have got to make the most of the moments you have in this life with your loved ones. I was so thankful that I was with a fellowship of people who believed in the power of prayer and that is certainly what kept us going.

Helen was to have her operation two days before Christmas, and we dropped Helen at Raigmore to get settled in the night before the operation. I and the children were staying for two nights in a Travelodge, and we held hands together to pray for Helen, and the children were asking if mum was going to be alright, we prayed that God would be with mum and bless her and bring her through the operation.

The next morning Helen went through the operation, and we heard about 11.00am that she was well and the procedure went very well.

We went to see Helen at tea-time, and she surprised us when we arrived by being ready with all her clothes on and saying I am staying the night in the hotel with you all. We were rejoicing!

Before she left we were to meet with the consultant who encouraged us by saying that the operation had gone really well and that the lump was smaller than what he had anticipated.

We were so thankful to the doctor and nurses for taking care of Helen and thankful to God to have mum come to the hotel with us.

I will never forget that Helen was shopping in Tesco at 11.00pm after going through a lumpectomy only 12 hours beforehand. What a woman!

God was very faithful in seeing us through this difficult time, but the next five years would have its challenges as Helen would have to go through six weeks of radiotherapy which meant leaving her young children behind, and having to stay at Raigmore from Monday to Friday but come home at weekends, this was a very tiring time for Helen and hard time for me and the children. We also had various check-ups and appointments over the years which were worrying as well until the great day arrived that she would no longer have to have so many check-ups just yearly mammograms!

Through those years I remember on one occasion we were at a meeting in Uig and Helen was prayed for with laying on of hands and one of our young worship leaders, Daniel Docherty sang the following words, 'Every little thing is going to be alright, every little thing is going to be alright.'

It was like a prophetic song sung over Helen from our loving heavenly Father who says in His word that He rejoices over us with singing.

We were facing another appointment at Raigmore, which was one of those frightening times to find out if the cancer had spread or not, and on the Sunday before the appointment, these were the words God gave us, through a young man who did not know what we were going through or going to face at the end of that week.

'Every little thing is going to be alright!' and thank God it was!

Over these uncertain years my ministry changed quite dramatically as I could certainly empathise with others who were going through similar health problems.

Our start at SBC had been not what I had expected, as I thought I would experience the Pentecostal blessing being with Spirit-filled Christians and having a good old Pentecostal knees up every Sunday and that all would be rosy in the garden.

I was reminded that life is not always like that, there are the valleys we have to go through before we reach the mountain tops, and I was bang in the middle of a valley that was hard to get out of, I certainly could not do it in my own strength but God was in the valley with us giving us His strength. I have often asked the question to God, 'Why?' And I look at the cross, and ask the question back to myself and say, 'Why?'

I found help and inspiration from Corrie Ten Boom, who ended up in a Nazi death camp with her sister Betsie, who died in that awful place. One evening Corrie was speaking at a church meeting, as she was speaking, she was also working on a piece of embroidery and as she talked and worked her needle back and forth, she was describing the plan that God had for our lives.

She talked about how her life had been lived in triumph and tragedy. She told of her prisoner-of-war camp experiences and the painful loss of her wonderful sister. Near the end of her talk, she held up the piece of cloth on which she was working to display the reverse side. It was nothing but a jumble of coloured threads, but she said that to us life often appears in a jumble. We can't seem to figure out what is happening or why God allows certain circumstances into our lives. Then she flipped the cloth over to show us a beautiful picture of a crown. This, Corrie said, is what God sees and what He working to complete in our lives. Then she concluded with the rendition of this poem:

My life is but a weaving,
between God and me
I do not choose the colours,
He worketh steadily

Oft times He weaveth sorrow,
and I in foolish pride,
Forget He sees the upper,
and I the underside.
Not till the loom is silent,
and the shuttles cease to fly
Will God unroll the canvas,
and explain the reason why,
The dark threads are as needful,
in the skillful Weaver's hand,
As the threads of gold and silver,
in the pattern He has planned.[1]

Life is difficult for all of us, no matter if we are a believer or an unbeliever, we all have our highs and lows, our sadness and joys, our trials and tribulations. Jesus reminded us of this in John 16:33 when He says: *"I have told you these things, so that in me you may have peace. In this world you will have trouble. But take heart! I have overcome the world."* As Christians we are not immune to the storms of life but thanks be to God that Jesus is in the boat with us.

Weeping may endure for a night but joy comes in the morning! It was longer than a night, but the day came when Helen received the good news that she was healed and clear of cancer.

---

[1] Moments for Mothers by Robert Strand.

What a relief! What joy! Praise the Lord!

8: TIMES OF REFRESHING

Our ministry continued at SBC and the youth work was going really well. Alistair and I met with Peter McDermott of FIG fellowship to pray and chat together.

Peter had been the co-ordinator of Skye Alive, which many Christians were involved in, it was a Christian worship and teaching conference that had happened for a number of years in Broadford, but had stopped. He felt that something was to start up again and asked to meet us for prayer, it was at that meeting God gave me a vision for an outreach event for our island.

It was to be evangelical and open to all

people and the churches would work together. What developed was an event called Refresh, which was a Christian music festival over a weekend with different outreach events, which happened on the last week before schools broke up for the summer holidays in June.

It seemed an awesome idea but I did not know of any bands or Christian singers to come and be involved and partner with us.

Then a door opened, I met Tim Cheshire who was lead singer of the band Superhero, and he and his band accepted an invitation to come and do some work in the High School and a Friday evening gig in the February before Refresh.

It was amazing having these cool Christians come into the High School to lead assemblies and share their faith, Portree had never seen the likes of it before. The gig went really well and Tim encouraged me to drive on with the Refresh festival in June and they would headline the event.

As the months passed I managed to get involved with Cuillin FM Radio station and I was given an hourly programme which I called Solid Rock, it was a mixture of testimonies and Christian contemporary music, which was incredible opportunity to have in a local radio station.

This programme helped me to interview lots of Christian bands and play their music and promote Refresh.

Our first Refresh festival was in June 2010 and we had a band from USA called Anchor of Hope, Malachi Christian punk rock band from Wales, we had an amazing rapper called MPFree (Marc Pawson) and a rock band Royal Foundlings, both from Glasgow.

We also had our own SBC youth band called Rendezvous, and Brian Irvine, Ross County footballer came and shared his testimony.

It was an awesome event as we reached into our community with the gospel. We started the weekend with an outdoor gig in Portree Square with all of these bands taking part, it was loud and the whole of Portree heard the gospel that evening.

The weekend went well although we did not get as many to the weekend as we hoped, nevertheless a few young people made commitments to Jesus Christ. We kept the momentum of Refresh going throughout the year by having local F5 (F5 = Refresh on the computer keyboard) gigs in the old library building about two in a year leading up to the next Refresh in 2011.

These smaller events were often

packed out with young people and our weekly youth outreach group on Friday nights were averaging 50 young people. Our second Refresh festival turned out to be the most successful in terms of people being saved, I cannot remember how many people gave their lives to Jesus over that weekend but it was certainly in double figures, and not all of them were young people.

From Refresh to Burnout

The ministry at SBC was all consuming to me and I was overdoing things. I also was having a lot of stress within the leadership meetings as people had different ideas about doing things and some were wanting to lead the church in a particular way. The eldership became a source of exhaustion to me and it was getting to the stage that I did not like going to these meetings and I was starting to resent some of the elders' decisions that they were making. It all became too much and I remember getting up one day and saying I cannot do this anymore. I am done in!

I was not sleeping, I was feeling physically ill with various ailments, and I was always tired and irritable. I had to make an appointment with my GP who was a

Christian and I shared with him how I was feeling and I started to cry. I did not have the strength to meet with people and in particular with my congregation, I did not have the energy or desire to listen to their hurts, I did not have the strength to preach the word, I was finding it difficult to concentrate on anything. My prayer life had dried up, my joy had gone, and I was a broken man.

My GP looked at me and said, 'I know what is wrong with you Gary, I have seen what minister's give out over the years, sweat, tears, everything, you are suffering from exhaustion. I want you to get away from Skye for at least two weeks, visit your Dad stay with him and get rest.'

That two weeks of rest lasted four months! The leaders and congregation were tremendous to me and my family and gave me paid leave for the duration of my time out.

It was during that time I was doing some serious soul searching as to what I had become from a so-called pillar of community to a burnt out wreck of a man.

Stress can subtly creep up on you without you being aware of it, until you have to stop what you are doing and seek help and support. Yes! God is my refuge and strength as the psalmist writes, a very present help in times of trouble. (Psalm 46). He was and is, but I had to recognise that for too long I had been running on my own strength which was hovering on the empty and I could not go on.

From Burnout to Refresh

God was very patient and gentle with me as I took time to adjust to the quiet life. Psalm 46 was a turning point for me in my time out, it says, *'Be still and know that I am God.'* God was asking no more or no less than to be still. I had been over busy in the past and did not take time out to be still, to my own detriment.

God now had my attention.

I was exhausted and He gently led me back to solitude, silence and healing as his word and Spirit touched my life afresh.

I heard the voice of Jesus say, 'Come unto me and rest, lay down thou weary one lay down, thy head upon my breast. I can to Jesus as I was weary, worn and sad. I found in Him a resting place and He has made me glad.'

Our God is the Lord of the Sabbath and my problem was that I had been too many Sabbath's in arrears. Alistair took on the role of pastor in my absence for which I will be eternally grateful that he was around, and it was he who made sure that I had the proper time and rest that I needed.

I gently started back about four months later, although still pretty fragile, and it was decided that I would minister at Glenelg fellowship for a period of time before I was back into the full swing of things. Glenelg fellowship are a small, Holy Spirit filled gathering, of a few families who have been worshipping the Lord in the village for almost 25 years. These dear brothers and sisters ministered to me, encouragement, love and peace. Although I was to bring God's word to them for a period of a few months, God ministered to me through these precious people. They helped to give me hope and confidence and renewal back into my life again. I thank God for Peggy the matriarch of the fellowship who is a wonderful spirit filled Christian and to this very day still so encouraging and uplifting every time I visit the fellowship.

The Lord has opened many doors for me to minister on Skye for the last 20 years from being a chaplain to seven different schools on the Island, being involved in football teams through playing for and sometimes coaching some of these young men, which has been a pleasure.

Having a programme on Cuillin FM, being interviewed by local and national papers proclaiming the good news of Jesus Christ. We have done street evangelism, singing, praying, dancing, drama sketches all for the glory of God. I have pastored, preached, laughed, cried, have had highs, lows, funerals, weddings, baptisms, salvations, in the name of Jesus. It is a privilege and blessing still to be involved in people's lives, sharing the love of Jesus in many diverse situations and among so many different people.

9: IMMANUEL – GOD WITH US

I want to finish with an incredible experience that happened to me one Christmas time a few years ago. I was in my study trying to prepare a word for Christmas Day service, I was praying asking God what He wanted me to share. God impressed on my heart that I was to speak about Immanuel which is a Hebrew name for God which means: 'God with Us.' As I started to write down my thoughts, I was reminded of how used to attend a prayer meeting in Glasgow which was led by a Jewish lady called Hansie Douglas (which was her married name), she had written her life story under her family name of Johanna Ruth Dobschiner called, *Selected to Live*.

This story was of how her Jewish childhood was ravaged by the Nazis in the Second World War and how she witnessed the total destruction of her family, even as she miraculously escaped from the clutches of evil. I wanted to quote from this book and I was looking everywhere in my house for my copy. I could not find it.

The reason I wanted to quote was within the book she tells of how God revealed Himself as Immanuel while she had contracted Scarlet Fever. I must have lent the book to someone.

It was a few days before Christmas and I had arranged to meet a couple in the Red Brick Café in Portree. As I was chatting with this couple, out of the corner of my eye, my attention was drawn to a woman across at another table from me and she was reading a book, I thought this odd, as usually people are on their phones nowadays. I was intrigued and I could make out the book was 'Selected to Live' and my heart almost missed a beat. I looked away and thought I must be seeing things, no for sure it was the book I was looking for. I tried to finish my conversation with the couple I was with, and we eventually said our good-byes. By the time I looked across at where the woman had been sitting, she was still there but the book had been put away.

I started to doubt myself, but then I thought what harm is there in asking if she had been reading the book. This lady was a stranger to me, I went over and introduced myself and she said, 'I know of you. You went to a prayer meeting in Glasgow that my mum was involved in with Hansie Douglas, and you also prayed with my mum in Safed in Israel when you visited there.'

Her mum was called Isabel who I knew quite well. I asked,

'Were you reading 'Selected to Live?'

'Yes!'

I told her of my dilemma and how I could not find my copy and wanted to quote from it. She handed it to me. I said it might take me a wee while to find the page. As I opened it, she had her book mark in the page where she had finished her reading, it was page 54 and as I looked at it, the word IMMANUEL leapt out at me. It was the page I had wanted to quote from!

I quote: "It was there in that bedroom, while blessed with Scarlet Fever, that a mighty truth suddenly penetrated my whole being. It was like a message from on high, a strange experience indeed. I was awed and full of joy and gratitude. The experience expressed itself in three words. These gave me strength for the next two years.

Through the wildest and most dreadful events, these three words were to be my reality and assurance.

Over and over I repeated them in thought, even whispering them aloud. In December 1942, this remote person the Almighty God had allowed me a glimpse of Himself...I now knew that He was and is and would come again. Three words now stood rock-like in my life...'GOD... WITH... US!"

I cried out in the café, 'Hallelujah!' 'Praise the Lord!' I then asked the lady if she was living on Skye, and she replied that she was just passing through after having a meeting and had stopped off for a coffee before she headed back to Inverness. I was incredibly moved that I had just happened to be there at the right time, and I just happened to be needing to quote from a particular book and there are millions, upon millions of books in the world, and it just happened that she was reading the book I needed and of all the 256 pages of the book she just happened to have it marked at the page I needed to quote from.

I was sure that the Lord wanted me to give the Christmas message that year on IMMANUEL... GOD... WITH... US! People would call it a co-incidence but I don't, it was a God-incidence, which I have proclaimed over the past few years.

GOD WITH US is not just for Christmas it's for all times and all people who go through various challenges, trials, and tribulations in life. When the world was in great darkness God sent His Son, to be light and to be with us.

GOD WITH US takes from the old into the new, from the sorrow into joy, from brokenness to wholeness, from captivity to freedom!

My life has been a mixture of 'out with the old - in with the new.' It is not a one off event, it is a continuous working within one's life. For I am not the finished product in fact, I am a work in progress.

I thank the Lord for my precious family: Helen and Andrew, Sarah and Rachel. A special thanks to God for my loving wife and for the support and strength she has given me over the years and for the faith that shines through even in the darkest of times.

'Forget the former things; do not dwell on the past. See, I am doing a new thing! Now it springs up; do you not perceive it?'
(Isa. 43:18-19).

ABOUT THE AUTHOR

Gary Wilson has been a minister on the Isle of Skye for 20 years. He is married to Helen and has three children, Andrew, Sarah and Rachel. He plays football for a local team, and he presents a Christian music programme on Radio Skye. He is also a sports chaplain for his local shinty club.

Printed in Great Britain
by Amazon